The Notation Is Not the Music

PUBLICATIONS OF THE
EARLY MUSIC INSTITUTE

Paul Elliott, editor

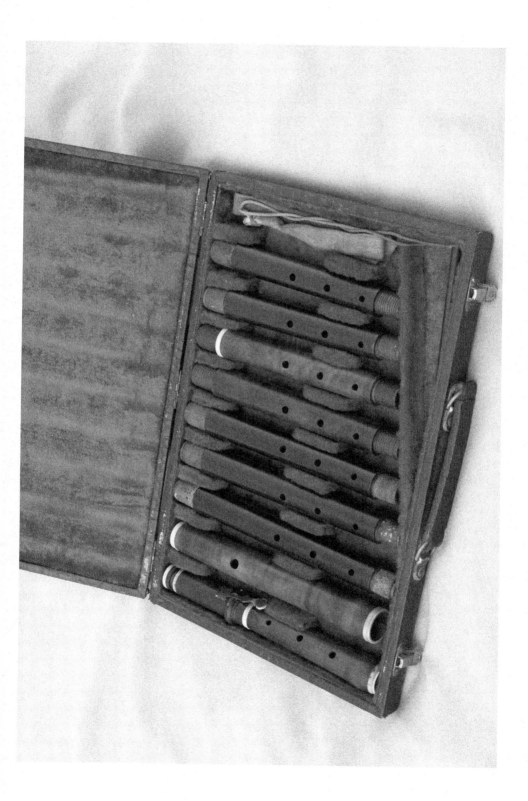

The Notation Is Not the Music

Reflections on Early Music Practice and Performance

Barthold Kuijken

INDIANA UNIVERSITY PRESS

Bloomington & Indianapolis

This book is a publication of

INDIANA UNIVERSITY PRESS
Herman B Wells Library 350
1320 East 10th Street
Bloomington, Indiana 47405 USA

iupress.indiana.edu

Telephone orders 800-842-6796
Fax orders 812-855-7931

KONINKLIJK
CONSERVATORIUM
BRUSSEL

With the generous support of the
Brussels Conservatory

∞ The paper used in this publication
meets the minimum requirements of
the American National Standard for
Information Sciences–Permanence of
Paper for Printed Library Materials,
ANSI Z39.48–1992.

*Manufactured in the
United States of America*

*Library of Congress
Cataloging-in-Publication Data*

Kuijken, Barthold, author.
  The notation is not the music : reflec-
tions on early music practice and
performance / Barthold Kuijken.
    pages cm — (Publications of the
Early Music Institute)
  Includes bibliographical references
and index.
  ISBN 978-0-253-01060-5 (cloth : alka-
line paper) — ISBN 978-0-253-01068-1
(ebook)
  1. Performance practice (Music) I.
Title. II. Series: Publications of the
Early Music Institute.
  ML457.K75 2013
  781.4'3—dc23

                    2013018439

1 2 3 4 5   18 17 16 15 14 13

I dedicate this book to the memory of my parents:
> I still see how they sat in our concerts, listening, participating, enjoying ...

to my wife Michèle:
> for having allowed me the time and space to follow my artistic path
> for having such a loving, attentive and critical ear
> for having taught me to look in the mirror.

With thanks to:

Prof. Dr. Hans De Wolf (VUB), former director of the Brussels Platform of the Arts, and the staff of the Brussels Royal Conservatory, for encouragement and practical assistance;

Barbara Kallaur, for the patient and dedicated editing of my English text.

Do not try to find the footprints of the ancestors,
search for what they were searching for.

—MATSUO BASHO (1644–1694)

CONTENTS

PREFACE

This essay is not meant to be a musicological study nor a practical how-to-play Early Music guide with detailed references to all the historical sources; enough examples of both kinds already exist. I very deliberately chose to include an index of only the most relevant composers and concepts. I also refrained from using an extensive bibliographic footnote apparatus; instead, I cite my main sources in Sources of Inspiration and the bibliography, or refer to specific publications at the beginning of some sections. Indeed, scholarly footnotes (mostly quoting well-known facts, historical treatises, or more recent musicological studies) generally lift the information out of its context and refer to isolated facts rather than pointing to the general principles and underlying aesthetic attitude. Further, I do not want to use the weight of their authority in order to prove anything—in art nothing can or needs to be proven. Instead I wish to reflect upon the ideas behind the facts, behind the theory and practice of Early Music as I have participated in them, and as I should like to pass them on to future generations of musicians.

My theoretical research and my practical research have always influenced and inspired each other. The former enables me to learn about the performance conventions and sound ideals of a given place and time, while the latter consists of finding and learning to play the "right" instrument, or to translate these ideals into actual sound. I did not follow a premeditated path, but let myself be driven by necessity, as questions popped up during playing, conducting, teaching, or studying treatises and musicological studies.

I have always considered my research to be "artistic research" even before this expression was coined. This kind of research is essentially both subjective and creative. Indeed, the artist as researcher does not stand beside or outside his topic, but is himself part of the researched topic—it is research in, not about, art. The results of this research are not aimed at being scientific; they can be art just as well. Per definition, artistic research is never definitive nor complete. It cannot be exactly repeated and does not strive to prove something. It is never a goal in itself but leads to deeper understanding and thus, hopefully, to better performance or creation. The results needed to be practiced, technically and artistically mastered, applied and integrated in my own thinking, feeling, playing, conducting, and teaching, until they became part of my "mother tongue."

This essay thus inevitably expresses my own current brand of "common knowledge," practice and theory, and will be shaped and limited by the extent of my own research and performance experience. I hope that it can give occasion to extrapolation, that it might contribute to further thinking and searching by those who love Early Music, are intrigued by it, and desire to share this art form with their audiences.

I hope that female readers will accept my apologies for consistently using the masculine pronouns throughout the book. This was done, not as a discriminatory move, but for the sake of brevity and simplicity.

The Notation Is Not the Music

1

❧

THE UNDERLYING
PHILOSOPHY

❧

When reading most twentieth- or twenty-first-century scores, trained musicians can hear them quite precisely in their "mind's ear." The exact instrumentation is given; the characteristics of the instruments are familiar; standard modern pitch and equal temperament are presupposed; tempo is prescribed by metronome markings; rhythm, phrasing, articulation and dynamics are clearly indicated; the realization of the few ornament signs is obvious; even the playing techniques and sound colors are accurately notated. Except in pieces that include aleatoric composition techniques or improvisation, performers do not have much room for adding individual accents or textual changes. This adherence to the written text is exactly what many composers wanted. Consequently, this kind of traditionally notated composition can be studied quite accurately from the score.

In earlier compositions, one easily notices that some notational parameters seem to be absent, whereas others have a less compelling or altogether different meaning that is dependent upon the time or place of composition. Their "correct" performance cannot be documented through personal acquaintance with the composer or his contemporaneous performers, nor by studying original sound recordings. This is the repertoire I shall address as "Early Music."

However, Early Music is not only a particular repertoire, but it is also understood as including Historically Informed Performance. In my eyes, this should not be a goal in itself. It is rather an attitude, a way of reading and rendering a score, striving for historical authenticity and at the same time taking up one's full responsibility as a performer. It certainly does not consist of easy-to-learn fixed sets of rules.

We should bear in mind that in actual performance musicians were often required to add their own unique layer of interpretation, which could or even should be different each time the work was played. Without this essential and creative performer-provided contribution, the audience would hear an incomplete piece. Thus, studying an Early Music score according to present-day reading conventions, without mentally including the performer's layer of interpretation, means studying an incomplete and thus different piece and coming to incomplete and thus different conclusions. This danger is encountered in musicology as well as in performance.

The fact that in Early Music there is no longer direct access to the composer's original creative concept can lead to absolute arbitrariness and neglect of even the most obvious historical information about topics such as instrumentation, ornamentation, tempo, rubato, et cetera. The composition is then often used as a pretext for displaying the performers' own ideas, emotions, and virtuosity. Regrettably, this also sometimes happens under the commercially successful label of "authentic Early Music on Historical Instruments." The (mostly) non-specialist audience is generally not able to detect the degree of conscious or unconscious manipulation involved, and sure enough, the performance can be very captivating. Alternatively, the wealth of historical documentation about the performance of Early Music can be studied, integrated, and put into practice. Such performances need not be less captivating for being better informed. However, it will be immediately clear that we shall never know, for example, exactly how J. S. Bach played (on which day?). All we can aspire to do is to fall reasonably well within the limits of probability and *good taste.*

The great artistry, charisma, pedagogical authority, and commercial success of some Early Music performers can be dangerous as well.

Audiences, colleagues, and students all too readily accept that these "stars" know all about Early Music, and so their performance is taken as a model to unthinkingly imitate. Needless to say, we thus create a new performance tradition that is based on the personal choice of some historical facts plus a strong dose of individual genius. In doing so, we remove ourselves one step away from the historical documentation itself. Students of these "stars" will tend to imitate them, rather than study the facts that shaped the teachers' decision—and so it goes to the third generation and the students beyond. This evolution is clearly visible and audible. It is the price we pay for the success of Early Music in concerts, publications, and recordings, the price we pay for having Early Music courses in most major conservatories. I think this can never be completely avoided; imitation is, at least temporarily, a part of the artistic learning process, but I consider it the teacher's task to leave this developmental stage as soon as possible.

These two problems, arbitrariness and alienation from the sources themselves, usually go hand in hand and can become fashion; indeed, some Early Music performers are proud to "emancipate" themselves from the sources. I would call this the "modern" Early Music tradition. Interestingly, in many cases this approach uses successful recipes of late-romantic performance practice, such as extended crescendos and diminuendos, upbeat phrasing, continuous vibrato, and modern rubato. Compositions are often subjected to re-instrumentation and arrangement in order to make them more "interesting" or to blow up their length. What I call the "Bolero effect" has become very popular. The formula is as follows: start with a percussion instrument solo, then add the bass, then one more voice, until everybody is playing, and, if desired, do the same in reverse order at the end. All these devices are easy to apply and do not require much specialized knowledge or technique. They benefit from being familiar or easy to understand for today's average listener, which also explains the success of this kind of performance. In itself this is not a problem; every performer is free to do as he wishes. However, when these performances are being advertised under the false label of "authentic Early Music," either explicitly or implicitly, I perceive this as some kind of intellectual and artistic fraud.

What might be an alternative? We cannot go back to the situation in the 1950s and 1960s, where one was virtually obliged to be self-taught, because formal instruction in Early Music was rarely available. I do not wish to turn the clock back, but rather desire to profit from the immense availability of information, which then needs to be taken seriously, studied, digested, and applied. There is also a need for diversification—the more we study the old sources, the more it becomes obvious that there is not a unique historical truth, valid for all times, places, styles, genres, and composers.

In my own teaching, I feel responsible for having my students focus on the historical source material itself: the scores, instruments, iconography, and treatises, rather than modern editions, replicas, translations, studies, and comments. Indeed, why should my students accept my interpretations of the historical material? Even with my best intentions, the information I hand them will be paraphrased, truncated, manipulated, chosen, neglected, or combined, and anyway subjected to my own biases, (in)capacities, experiences, blind spots, temperament, and taste. Students must be taught to view all information, be it from their music teachers or from musicology, with a critical eye and a healthy dose of skepticism. In my opinion, and not only in the field of Early Music, any teacher's goal is to make himself superfluous and train his students to become autodidacts. As artists, teachers as well as students need to acquire and maintain their instrumental or vocal mastery and simultaneously become and stay well informed, and let these two areas of study fruitfully interact with each other. I realize this is not the fast and easy way, neither for students nor for teachers, but it is certainly most rewarding for both. The benefit will be for their audiences, who will not be fooled by the Emperor's new clothes.

2

❦

MY WAY TOWARD
RESEARCH

❦

My passion for Early Music developed in the 1960s. I played the recorder in childhood and continue to play it, with much pleasure, as
a secondary instrument next to the transverse flute. Contrary to the
opinion of my flute teacher at music school, who saw the recorder as
a mere toy or penny whistle, I could not help but consider it as a real
instrument. Since there was nobody around to teach me the recorder
on a regular basis, I had to proceed alone. This autodidactic approach
became second nature, and I profoundly enjoyed inventing every next
move myself. In this I was greatly supported by the general family
spirit of curiosity and independent thinking, also (especially?) when
this went against institutions and authorities such as school or tradition. As children we were encouraged to follow our own path but were
reminded by our parents of the risk of doing so. In other words, if you
were convinced, go ahead, but do not complain afterward about the
consequences.

I was stimulated by the presence of my two older musician brothers, Wieland and Sigiswald, who were then having their first experiences with early string instruments. Unlike them, I had chosen
wind instruments, and this gave me a field of my own to cultivate.
I am very grateful to them for not having pushed me in any particu-

lar direction. At that time we were discovering and discussing the revolutionary recordings of musicians such as Alfred Deller, Nikolaus Harnoncourt, and Gustav Leonhardt. I remember I received Johann Joachim Quantz's famous *Versuch einer Anweisung, die Flöte traversiere zu spielen* (1752), one of the most influential eighteenth-century treatises, for my thirteenth birthday. I read it eagerly, learning German language and Gothic print along the way. I consider this to be the start of my (now already more than fifty years long) Early Music adventure. Quantz's book opened up a new world for me, and I was impatient to know more. Soon after, I was to become acquainted with other important treatises.

Just before entering the Brussels Royal Conservatory, I found my first "baroque" one-keyed flute (eventually I found out that it had been made in the mid-nineteenth century as a cheap model and constructed only partly according to eighteenth-century principles). It was not very good, but good enough to guide my first steps, and it made me hungry for more. I had already noticed that much of the flute repertoire before ca. 1750 sounded more appropriate to me on the recorder than on the modern flute, and now, even with this mediocre instrument, things fell into place, and felt natural (whatever that means). While studying at the Brussels Royal Conservatory, I discovered that its library was full of highly interesting scores and theoretical books, most of them then not yet republished, and I spent as much time as possible in this gold mine. This occurred parallel to, and independently of, my regular Boehm (modern) flute studies, which I enjoyed very much as well.

A decisive event happened during my first year at the conservatory; I found a splendid original flute—an incredible piece of luck for a boy of eighteen!—made in Brussels around 1750 by Godefroy Adrien Rottenburgh, one of the great woodwind instrument makers of the eighteenth century. Again, I had to proceed as an autodidact, since nobody was around to teach me the baroque flute. This proved to be a blessing—I had to make all mistakes myself and to discover by myself that (and why) they were mistakes. It was a slow learning process, but my good old flute was to become the best teacher I ever had. As really good instruments do, it showed me how it wanted (or did not want) to be played. Of course I continued my Boehm flute studies, simultaneously taking two years of art history at Ghent University. Following that, I studied for one year in Holland, focusing on contemporary Boehm flute repertoire. This should hardly be a surprise as contemporary music, just like music before Bach or Handel, was largely ignored (or ridiculed) at the conservatory, and this greatly stimulated my interest. In contemporary, often experimental, music, as in Early Music, and more than in the typical conservatory repertoire, the active and creative participation of the performer is required, and in the sixties and seventies many colleagues were simultaneously focusing on old and very new music, both left and right from the mainstream repertoire. But I felt that Early Music was my real passion, and during the following years, modern flute and contemporary repertoire gradually receded into the background.

My interest in research was prompted by those areas of my musical training (both at an early stage and at an advanced level) that seemed to contradict each other. Some examples:

- We were more or less explicitly expected to have perfect pitch, officially based on $a^1 = 440$ Hz, but modern orchestras played much higher, and old instruments could deviate from this by as much as a whole tone up and down.

- We learned that the major second consisted of the chromatic semitone (such as F—F♯), five commas wide, plus the diatonic semitone (F♯—G) of four commas, but in actual playing we had to make all semitones equal, as on the modern piano. However, treatises such as Quantz's *Versuch einer Anweisung* (1752) showed that in the seventeenth and eighteenth centuries the diatonic semitone was mostly considered to be wider than the chromatic, and that keyboards were seldom tuned with twelve equal semitones to the octave.

- In theory lessons we were shown the metrical realization of appoggiaturas (it was, astonishingly, basically the same theory as formulated in most of the eighteenth century), but in playing Bach or Mozart, we were not expected to apply these rules.

- All trills were to be started on the main note, but eighteenth-century treatises taught to start them from the upper note.
- Solfège and instrumental technique aimed at a literal, precise reading and rendering of the notation. Rhythmic freedom was not encouraged; I suppose this was judged too romantic for the post–World War II *neue Sachlichkeit* (New Objectivity). Historical treatises such as Quantz or Hotteterre, on the contrary, showed that the shortest note values in a given piece were frequently treated with considerable freedom and that rubato did not have the same meaning as today.
- I wondered why we did not analyze baroque or classical music according to eighteenth-century principles rather than using uniformly Schenkerean theory or functional harmony.

Further, the information I had begun to glean from historical treatises and instruments showed me how much standards and traditions changed over time. However, I did not hear or learn a substantially different approach in sound production, phrasing, or articulation according to different eras or countries: Vivaldi, Bach, Mozart, Beethoven, Wagner, Brahms, Debussy, Hindemith, Prokofiev, or Britten were all subjected to a rather uniform post-romantic interpretation. This was illustrated by many "modern" editions of, for example, J. S. Bach's music—they were freely annotated by well-known and well-meaning virtuosos, without specifying how the original text read. On the other hand, the existence of several *different* Urtext editions of one and the same work demonstrated the necessity of seeing the original sources myself, in order to make up my mind autonomously. In some cases, this later led me to publishing one more—again different—Urtext edition.

I could not understand how baroque music, as it was frequently played before the Early Music revival, could be so mechanical, straightforward, unemotional, even simplistic, compared with baroque paintings, statues, literature, or architecture. I wondered which role music played in the different layers of society, and how its features would vary according to its function. I also felt the need to examine the positioning of the performer between the composer and the audience, varying according to the nature of the piece to be performed. It became increasingly easy to find historical recordings by famous singers and actors, conductors, pianists, violinists, flautists, from the first half of the twentieth century. Many were reissued, first on LP, later on CD; YouTube and the Library of Congress's "National Jukebox" now make an overwhelming amount of historical sound and/or image information readily available for study. These recordings showed me how fast aesthetics, style, and fashion can change. I discovered a generally much freer and more varied approach to dynamics, tempo, and rubato, less ultimate precision in playing together, and much less scrupulous fidelity to the musicological/scientific model of (Ur)text. These recordings demonstrate highly prominent individual virtuosity and artistic presence. This reinforced my conviction that performance in earlier times might have been very different from today's standards indeed. Questioning traditions and conventions thus became a habit, and research became a vital necessity.

Initially my research focused on the baroque flutes and recorders, as played from ca. 1660—the first appearance of baroque recorders at the court of Louis XIV, where the one-keyed baroque flute arrived some twenty years later—until the end of the eighteenth century when multi-keyed flutes became widely adopted. Soon after, I started studying the instruments, performance practice, and repertoire of the nineteenth and early twentieth centuries. Occasionally I extended my research into Renaissance flutes and recorders and their repertoire. Purely theoretical books and treatises for other instruments provided me with the general framework in which to integrate the flute. After all, the flute and the recorder are not such important instruments! Much more was written about the voice, the violin, and the keyboard.

It became obvious to me that a general historical-artistic truth cannot exist and that every performer's conclusions inevitably depend on one's individual choices, driven by one's own artistic temperament, and made within the context of acquired historical knowledge. Research further helped me to understand the sound behind (or before) the notation and pointed to the necessity of "creative reading"; namely, learning to supplement what was not written. Even in the best situations, when this is done with respect for style and the genre and character of the music, we can only operate within a field of probabilities with fluctuating boundaries. I understood better and better that the very concept of authenticity in Early Music is considerably less clear or simple than it might appear at first sight.

As a result of my research I considered the notation to be mainly a type of roadmap, an *aide-mémoire* and help for invention, enabling the informed reader to create an inner image of the music. Quite naturally, this image is not definitive, but will change with time, mood, circumstance, and knowledge. Once this provisional image has been formed, in great detail, I can let it take an audible shape. In other words, I have to begin to play (or practice!) with the result clearly in my heart and mind. From this total concept, quasi-retrospectively and in constant interaction with the actual reading and playing, I shape my interpretation and determine all its performance parameters. In this sense, "early" music does not exist: the performance becomes a re-creation, the music is born at this very moment, the ink is still wet.

3

THE LIMITS OF
NOTATION

Notating everything with utmost precision, if possible at all, would ask for a very great effort and look very complicated. It would also limit the performer's freedom more than most performers or even composers would have wanted. In *Der Critische Musicus* (May 15, 1737), Johann Adolf Scheibe criticizes J. S. Bach's habit of writing out the whole "method" of playing, with much elaborate ornamentation, as being confusing to the reader. This is quite understandable, though from our point of view, we might have wished that Bach had been even more precise. Neither Scheibe nor Bach could have imagined that the generally scanty notation of earlier centuries would cause us so many problems and endless discussions today.

The desire to write down music as precisely as possible seems to be a typical concern of our Western "classical" music, culminating in the twentieth century. Schoenberg is quite radical in the preface to *Pierrot Lunaire* op. 21 (written in 1912, first published in 1914): the performer should not add anything that is not written down. He should give no interpretation of the music, "Er würde hier nicht geben, sondern nehmen" (he would not give, but take away). Stravinsky is not less compelling when he states (as reported by Robert Craft in *Conversations with Igor Stravinsky* [1959]) that his music must be read and executed, and not interpreted. Similarly in 1924, he wrote of his *Octet* that "to interpret a piece is to realize its portrait, and what I demand is the realization of the piece itself and not of its portrait." The extremely complex notation of many Boulez compositions can be considered as the logical consequence of this attitude. In the last third of the twentieth century, many composers reacted against this by developing aleatoric notation, graphic notation, and so forth. Sometimes the performers are requested to improvise instead of being given a fully written-out part.

Music can easily exist without notation, as we can see in other traditions, such as jazz, folk music, Gregorian chant, and Eastern music, where notation, if extant, is very incomplete and sketchy. Fundamentally, notation directs itself toward the wrong physical sense: toward the eye instead of the ear. We could paraphrase the German proverb, "Erzählte Musik ist wie ein gemaltes Mittagessen" (narrated music is like a painted meal) as "Notierte Musik ist wie ein gemaltes Mittagessen" (notated music is like a painted meal); we will stay hungry indeed! But where there is no extant living aural tradition, as in Early Music, the visual tradition has to suffice. However, this eye-notation must be decoded, and all too easily supposing that this decoding has been done in an identical way in all times and places leads us to wrong interpretations. Luckily, historical treatises do give us important decoding tools. As one would expect, the information is not unanimous, but it can put us on the right track; conversely, we might learn how the notation should not be read.

Anyway, the eye-notation must be completed by the aural experience. In performance, I continuously have to deal with fundamental questions such as: How does the hall sound? How will I integrate what comes into what I just played? What are my colleagues playing together with me? One practical consideration that is easily overlooked in today's theory and practice is the presence or absence of a complete score. Orchestral musicians always played from their separate parts, but after all, they were guided by a conductor or leader. However, if the leader is the Konzertmeister or the soloist of a concerto, he might never have possessed or seen a full score of the composition he is performing. The same applies to chamber music, where many pieces circulated only in handwritten separate parts. If printed, string quartets, for instance, were only sold in separate parts, until well into the nineteenth century. One had to wait for the complete edition of the works of the "great" classical or romantic composers, before seeing their quartets in score. Mozart's ten famous quartets appeared in score in 1828, shortly after Beethoven decided to have his last six quartets published in score as well as in parts (they were issued in 1826–27). He must have been one of the first to do so. Similarly he seems to have been one of the first to include letters in the score and parts, in order to facilitate rehearsing (among the quartets, they only appear in the *Große Fuge* op. 133, published in 1827). Did he consider these late works so complicated that the performer would need a score and, in the case of the *Große Fuge,* even letters? Bar numbers were generally included only in the second half of the twentieth century. Obviously, rehearsing must have been very different, without the help of bar numbers, letters, or even a score.

When most larger-scale compositions could not be studied through the eyes, only well-educated and experienced ears could tell how to react to what colleagues were playing. The performer had to trust his ears and to "feel" ahead—how did his playing need to be shaped by the other parts' consonances or dissonances, parallel motion or counterpoint, rhythmic shape, ornaments, dynamics, phrasing, and articulation? The performer also had to trust his colleagues' similar intuition, initiative, invention, and experience. This practice teaches the performers to listen to each other very intently; it might also have resulted in greater spontaneity and less ultimate "togetherness," as can be witnessed in recordings from the first half of the twentieth century. In the same vein, most early orchestral and chamber music parts conspicuously lack handwritten indications of bowings, fingerings, dynamics, or ornaments. Were these details remembered through rehearsals, or did they matter less?

Even if a composition is notated with the utmost care and precision, it is not going to be performed or heard the same way twice, either voluntarily or involuntarily. Both the playing and the listening environment keep changing. By its very nature, art is not repeatable. Even where the material form can be repeated (film, CD, multiple viewings of the same painting, repeated reading of the same book), the moment of the artistic experience, for both the creator and his public, is unique and cannot be fixed in its multiple layers of meaning. This essence, the emotional impact, can only be experienced in the here and now and cannot be fully replicated for perpetuity in notated form. In music, historical treatises seem to be well aware of this mutability and accept it. They stress that we must faithfully respect the intentions of the composer, and at the same time they emphasize that we are expected to add our personal share of invention. Obviously, the latter was also part of the composer's intention (or at least the composer's expectation), but it is not always clear to what degree. We can be guided by the many descriptions of great performers (but there again: "erzählte Musik . . ."). Descriptions of bad examples mainly criticize excesses, and, less often, under-interpretation such as lack of ornamentation. Criticisms such as those found in Bollioud de Mermet's *De la corruption du goust dans la musique françoise* (1746) might tell us as much about their author as about the performers he describes. Even so, they give us some detailed, albeit subjective, information.

Good taste is a key concept in many eighteenth-century treatises, being the sine qua non of artistry. Taste greatly influenced the way a composition was read—good taste in Versailles was not necessarily the same in Naples, London, or Berlin, not even in contemporaneous times. What was applauded in one place could be despised in another. The specific meaning of good taste must have been clear enough for the author himself or for his immediate surroundings, but the definition obviously varied greatly in time and place. To a certain extent, historical treatises can show us these changes of taste, but we have to be aware that the distance in time might cause a difference in our appreciation of a given idea. This can easily be experienced by listening to recordings from the beginning of the twentieth century. I propose to approach them with a very open mind, not with a retro attitude (in grandmother's time everything was better), but not with a condescending attitude, either. These recordings by universally acclaimed performers (who presumably possessed good taste) often sound foreign to us. Though they obviously read the same notation as we do, it is not easy to understand the musical choices and identify, for example, with Adelina Patti's rubato and glissandi in Mozart's *Voi che sapete,* Rachmaninov's beautifully free tempo in a Bach sarabande, or Mengelberg's dramatic *Matthäus Passion.* I can hardly imagine that still-earlier performing styles would sound more familiar to us!

4

THE NOTATION, ITS PERCEPTION, AND RENDERING

In sections 1–13 the most important notation parameters of Early Music will be treated separately. Short texts in italics will point to the frequent overlapping and continual cross-influence between them or will lead from one section to the next in an attempt to see all these parameters not as isolated elements, but rather as interwoven parts of one integral artistic product. In sections 14–18 some aspects will be treated that have a profound impact on the way the notation is read, received, and rendered to the audience.

Tuning and temperament have an immediate impact on the listener's ears. Research has shown that traditions and standards—and thus also their appreciation—have changed very much over the years. They kept changing until today, though through the introduction of electronic tuning devices, uniformity and repeatability are favored. I am not sure that this must be considered a gain.

1. PITCH

(All Hz figures should be understood as "ca."; especially for the organ, the influence of the church temperature should not be neglected.)

Much of the factual information upon which this section is based can be found in Bruce Haynes, *A History of Performing Pitch* (2002), to which I contributed many pitch data of historical flutes and recorders. Haynes's conclusions coincide with my own research and experience.

For most listeners, other than those with perfect pitch, centered at today's official $a^1 = 440$ Hz, hearing a piece lower or higher might not make very much difference, though the general mood and sound color will undoubtedly be changed. In earlier times there was no standard pitch. Around 1700–1750, Paris and Rome were reputed to play at a very low pitch ($a^1 = 392$ Hz), Venice and Lombardy at a very high pitch ($a^1 = 466$ Hz), with many German cities in between ($a^1 = 415$ Hz). Even within the same city the pitch could vary from one institution to another. In Berlin, ca. 1750, the opera and church pitch ($a^1 = 415$ Hz) was half a tone sharper than the pitch used by Frederick the Great ($a^1 = 392$ Hz). One can easily imagine the practical problems for performers playing for both the opera/church and at court. For traveling musicians, this was of constant concern. Similarly, makers had a difficult time supplying performers with adequate instruments for these challenging conditions. But it could be even more complicated; in Weimar and Leipzig, J. S. Bach used two different pitch standards simultaneously. In Weimar, the organ, singers, and string instruments used the high organ pitch ($a^1 = 466$ Hz, a semitone above 440 Hz), but the woodwinds used the French opera pitch ($a^1 = 392$ Hz, a minor third below the organ), and were thus notated transposed into another key. In Leipzig, the organ was tuned at the same high pitch, but the other instruments and the voices used a pitch of a^1 = 415 Hz, one tone lower. Here the organ had to transpose one tone down, which could cause severe intonation problems. For example, E-flat-major, which sounds quite well in the usual unequal temperament, now becomes a rather disastrous D-flat-major (see also the section about temperament below). Some organs had one stop tuned at a^1 = 415 Hz, in order to avoid these transpositions.

It is striking that the above-mentioned pitches all lie a semitone apart (from a^1 = 392 to a^1 = 415, to a^1 = 440, to a^1 = 466 Hz). This however, is an over-simplification and generalization of the state of affairs in the seventeenth and eighteenth centuries. In the twentieth century, semitone transposition was developed in order to accommodate today's harpsichords and organs, where the keyboard can be moved one or two halftones up or down. This moveable keyboard gradually came into use from around 1960. In the seventeenth and eighteenth centuries, few instruments possessed this device, although the keyboard of at least one of the Silbermann fortepianos at Frederick the Great's court could be moved by a semitone. This indicates that at the Potsdam court the pitch could vary, too.

Recorders and flutes did not substantially change pitch during their years of use and over the many more years of lying dormant in attics, museums, or collections. These instruments are a good guide toward establishing local and/or temporal pitch standards. However, we have to take into consideration that not all players produce the same pitch on a given instrument and that the ambient temperature also plays its role. Not unexpectedly, we find a wide array of pitches. Flutes were often made with several middle joints of different lengths. The resulting pitches usually lie about one or two commas apart from each other. My own G. A. Rottenburgh flute has seven middle joints in steps of ca. 8 mm, playing at a^1 = 392, 398, 404, 410, 416, 423, and 430 Hz (see plates). This instrument was stained dark, but the stain wears off where touched by lip or hand. Thus I could conclude that middle joint nr. 5 (at a^1 = 416 Hz), and to a lesser extent nr. 4 (at a^1 = 410 Hz), had been used most often: nr. 5 had the same stain color as the head joint and right hand joint; nr. 4 was somewhat darker still. The other middle joints obviously had been played very seldom. I made similar observations on some flutes that Quantz made for Frederick the Great. Here the color did not change (they are made in blackwood), but on five of the six middle joints the edges of the finger holes are still neat and sharp, whereas on the longest middle joint (at $a^1 =$ 392 Hz) they are rounded off, showing the same wear as on the right hand joint. This indicates that Frederick played most often at this very low pitch, a fact that is confirmed in Quantz's *Versuch*. Using a longer middle joint is often a better solution than lengthening the instrument by pulling out between head and middle joint, but both pulling out and choosing a longer or shorter middle joint for playing at lower or higher pitches change the proportions of the flute's inner bore, and thus cause tuning problems. The best solution is a completely new instrument, adequately designed for the desired pitch. Recorders did not use multiple middle joints, probably because their playing properties do not allow the same degree of pitch correction as the flute; oboes were made with up to three upper joints because their playing technique allows for easier pitch adjustments.

Today's listeners have become accustomed to hearing J. S. Bach's cantatas at $a^1 = 415$ rather than at 440 Hz, but they might still be astonished to hear the Weimar cantatas in their original set-up— simultaneously the string instruments are rather shrill and penetrating at $a^1 = 466$ Hz (with the same string thicknesses as for lower pitches?), the woodwinds quite dark at $a^1 = 392$ Hz, and the voices singing in a higher part of their register. During the last third of the previous century the acceptance of the $a^1 = 415$ Hz pitch for Bach cantatas took some time, and there was vehement opposition from many sides. I see this opposition as part of a zealous kind of self-defense put up by the "traditional camp." Unfortunately, the word "camp" was justified in those days; there was a deep separation and strong opposition between the traditional attitude and the historically informed attitude toward performance practices. Lower pitch was an easily identifiable feature of the totally different approach to Early Music in general and J. S. Bach in particular. As a pars pro toto it was attacked in defense of the "holy" Bach and the traditional performing style. I am very glad that this fanaticism, which existed on both sides, generally has made room for more understanding and respect. But some of these attitudes survive, even in a quite extreme form. Since the 1970s, Gérard Zwang has fulminated against differentiated lower or higher pitches and authentic instruments, and he continues to do so in writings such as *Guide pratique des Cantates de Bach* (1982) and more recently *Le Diapason* (1998). For him, the $a^1 = 440$ Hz standard is as immutable as the meter and the hour, in spite of all historical evidence.

For many years (and not only for Bach), $a^1 = 415$ Hz has been adopted as the all-purpose high-baroque pitch, though quite different standards can be documented for Lully, Couperin, Rameau, Purcell, Handel, Corelli, Vivaldi, and so forth. Fortunately, instruments at other pitches are being made and used with increasing frequency, allowing performers to exploit their different sound properties. This is certainly interesting, but at the same time difficult, inconvenient, and expensive. Indeed, as a flautist I need to have at my disposal—and feel intimately familiar with—about ten different pre-Boehm flute types in order to cover the repertoire from Lully to Schubert. In practical concert life I need to make compromises. When playing a recital, I cannot have four or five differently pitched keyboard instruments on stage. On the other hand, for recordings and unaccompanied recitals, I gladly use this opportunity to play at different pitches.

During the eighteenth and early nineteenth centuries, the pitch rose steadily, at some places faster than at others. At the same time, and even within the same pitch standard, the "center of gravity" of the woodwind instrument tessitura was gradually shifted upward, and the composers used the instruments accordingly. I devised an easy method to find this center of gravity of a given piece or part: (1) each note of the instrument's chromatic scale receives a number, starting with 1 on the lowest note; (2) for each note, this figure is multiplied by the number of times it occurs in the piece; (3) the sum of all these results is divided by the total amount of notes; (4) the pitch corresponding to this average value can be identified by the numbers given to the chromatic scale. Thus, the center of gravity of J. S. Bach's *Solo pour la flûte traversière* BWV 1013 (possibly ca. 1720) lies between d^2

and d♯², and of the flute part of Mozart's D-major flute quartet KV 285 (1777) at g²: almost a semitone higher per decade!

Today much of the classical repertoire is played at a¹ = 430 Hz. I must confess that I am responsible for this. In 1981, La Petite Bande, led by my brother Sigiswald, recorded a series of Haydn symphonies as a first incursion into the classical style. These recordings were never released because the result was not satisfactory. The pieces were difficult for all of us. Sigiswald uncompromisingly required chin-off playing for the violins and violas, and among the woodwinds, most of us had inappropriate instruments belonging to an earlier period. The pitch (a¹ = 415 Hz) and, even more so, the center of gravity of these instruments was too low—it felt like a mezzo soprano trying to sing a soprano part. La Petite Bande's next classical-era project, in 1982, was Haydn's *Die Schöpfung* (1798), which was even more difficult, and absolutely out of reach for our earlier baroque-era woodwinds. I was given the task of finding out what needed to be done about this. In the German Early Music orchestra Collegium Aureum, created by the record label Deutsche Harmonia Mundi in 1962, and in which I played from 1970 to 1978, I had had some experience with later types of oboes and flutes, which were then, for convenience's sake, constructed at (or rather pushed up to) a¹ = 440 Hz. Their makers had attempted to find compromises between modern and old instruments, but the results were not very convincing. Anyway, according to the information that I found, their pitch was rather high. I thus decided that we had to stay away from these instruments: I did not want to take these mediocre hybrids as a model by only lengthening them a bit to play at a lower pitch. On the other hand, I had experienced the pitch in Vienna's Concentus Musicus, the ensemble around Nikolaus Harnoncourt. Their oboist used an original instrument at a¹ = 422 Hz; in order to match this pitch, some of the other woodwinds, copied more or less faithfully after original models at a lower pitch, were shortened by almost a centimeter, throwing off the balance in their tuning and in their sound quality. Clearly, we had to stay far enough above the a¹ = 422 pitch if we wanted to avoid cutting down flutes and oboes even further. So I chose, quite arbitrarily, a¹ = 430 Hz, in between 422 and 440. At that time I had a beautiful original flute on loan, made in the

1780s in Dresden by one of the greatest German flute makers, August Grenser. It had four middle joints, at a^1 = 427, 433, 437, and 442 Hz. A fifth middle joint at 430 Hz had to be made, and original oboes, clarinets, and bassoons had to be found and copied. Fortunately, with the brass instruments, the hitches created by lengthening or shortening the tube were less problematic. We all had to learn to play these new instruments in a very short amount of time. I led the first wind rehearsal; it started as a disaster and we might easily have been discouraged, but since the project was on its way, we soldiered on, and the live recording of the performance (Accent Live, 1982) is astonishingly good. Later studies showed me that at the time of Haydn's *Schöpfung,* pitches close to a^1 = 440 Hz as well as around a^1 = 422 Hz were in use; a^1 = 430 Hz is no more than an average, and has not been so frequently documented. After our recording project, these newly constructed and mastered instruments continued to be played and liked in several other period-instrument orchestras, so a^1 = 430 Hz became a practical compromise for traveling musicians worldwide. However, this solution should by no means be confused with historical truth or be considered as *the* historical pitch for classical music.

Temperament is a very personal and subjective matter, even though it has been dealt with in great detail by acousticians and mathematicians, with many (inaudible) decimal digits. Tuning by ear, hardly anybody will exactly duplicate the same temperament, even if wanting to do so. The difference between one tuner and another might be bigger still, and the sound properties of individual instruments can also have their influence upon the final result.

2. TEMPERAMENT

Mark Lindley gives a good overview of the different historical tuning systems in Howard Mayer Brown and Stanley Sadie (eds.), *The Norton/Grove Handbooks in Music: Performance Practice, Music after 1600* (1989).

Unfortunately, in any given composition, one cannot simultaneously have all octaves, fifths, fourths, and thirds—the first encountered intervals in the series of overtones—acoustically pure, i.e. non-beating against each other. Temperaments are practical solutions to this problem, necessitated by the fixed notes of the keyboard or the fixed position of the frets on lute or viola da gamba.

Each tuning system has its own characteristics, and thus its own expressive qualities, depending on the number and kind of pure or impure intervals. Quarter-comma meantone, often used in the seventeenth century, opts for pure major thirds, and that results in eleven very flat and one much too wide fifth (it is rather a diminished sixth: G♯—E♭). This temperament works quite well for pieces with no more than three or four sharps or flats, as was then customary. In the later seventeenth and eighteenth centuries, many systems were *wohltemperiert* (well-tempered), enabling one to play in all keys. However, this does not mean that all keys would sound identical; there could be a gradual favoring of pure fifths over pure thirds as one gets farther from C-major. Transposing a piece, then, is not just playing it lower or higher; the placement of notes within the octave, and thus the overall result, is different from one tonality to another. Within a piece, repeating a theme in another key can also make a noticeable difference. These differences are lost in equal temperament.

By the sixteenth century, some keyboard and lute players must have been frustrated when wanting to play with more than the customary three or four sharps or flats. It is no wonder that they were the first who occasionally refer to equal temperament as a solution. Shortly before 1600, Simon Stevin succeeded in presenting its mathematical structure. In equal temperament all fifths are slightly smaller and all major thirds are quite a lot wider than pure. As a result, all tonalities are identical. Though unequal tuning systems are still mentioned throughout the nineteenth century, equal temperament obviously became the best choice for the expanding harmonic language. It has stayed in use through today as a very practical compromise, even with the limitation that equal temperament contains no pure intervals. It is not, however, practical or particularly useful for Early Music.

The fact that keyboard instruments need one temperament or another does not necessarily mean that all other instruments and voices should be enslaved by the same rigors, certainly not in Early Music, with its relatively simple harmonies and strongly modal or tonal structure. String instruments are somewhat limited by their open strings: when both a cello and a violin tune all their fifths pure, the interval between the cello's lowest string (C) and the violin's highest string (e^2)—three octaves plus a major third—is much too wide. If they tune this interval pure, their fifths become very small. The rich overtones of a good string instrument include, of course, both the pure fifth and the pure major third, but we cannot have the best of both worlds, so usually string players will choose something in between these two extreme solutions. Fretted string instruments will naturally prefer equal or not-too-unequal temperament, since on the bass viol, for example, c♯ (low in quarter-comma meantone tuning) must be taken on the same fret as b♭ (high in quarter-comma meantone tuning). Brass instruments, lacking holes or valves, obviously use the pure harmonic overtones; any deviation from these, or notes not falling into the overtone series (when playable at all) must be achieved by lip and breath corrections. Woodwinds were not tuned in a specific system, but through fingering and embouchure (and good ears) they mostly could adapt quite well to different situations. The voice is the most adaptable and free; singing pure intervals gives a very resonant quality to an ensemble or choir, but might entail a subtle change of overall pitch during a piece. Indeed, let us suppose using pure thirds and fifths in a C-major a cappella piece. The A can be in a low position as a fifth below E, or in a high position as a fifth above D. It can be easily computed that the difference between these two positions is almost a quarter of an equally tempered semitone—quite noticeable! When the A is reached against an already sounding and held D or E, the singer or conductor has to choose between one of the two positions. If this A in its turn becomes a note against which other intervals have to be tuned, a substantial pitch variance can be noticed for the whole piece. Most performers would cheat, however, accepting a not-so-pure fifth D-A or A-E, or slightly vary the pitch of the tenuto D or E. In practice, the resonating quality of pure intervals is most important on long notes and at important places, whereas passing notes or dissonances can be treated more flexibly. Life is not perfect!

Simultaneous pitch standards, as in Bach's Weimar and Leipzig cantatas, cause some problems due to the involved transposition. In many unequal temperaments, D♭-major sounds less well than E♭-major because the D♭ is too low, rather functioning as a C♯. Consequently the major triad on the tonic of D♭-major is quite out of tune because of the much too wide major third between D♭ and F.

Historical treatises also mention the problems encountered when different types of instruments, each favoring a different temperament, play together. Not all problems can be avoided, but in practice, keyboard players could omit disturbing out-of-tune notes from their basso continuo realization, or hide them in the middle of the chord. Georg Falck, in his *Idea Boni Cantoris* (1688) recommends organists play a trill or mordent on an out-of-tune note (for example when F should function as E♯). Johann Georg Tromlitz, in his influential *Ausführlicher und gründlicher Unterricht die Flöte zu spielen* (1791), provides interesting information. He would like the keyboard to be tuned in equal temperament (though the method he describes will not really yield equal temperament), but recommends leaving out the keyboard from larger ensembles so that the other instruments can play pure thirds and fifths in the important chords. Furthermore, in *Ueber die Flöte mit mehrern Klappen* (1800), he shows that an a♯¹ as lower appoggiatura to the b♮¹ of the G-major triad G-B-D can be played higher, with the enharmonic b♭♮ fingering. The same can be applied to passing notes, neighbor notes, and so forth. I find this expressive tuning of non-essential notes highly efficient, but not many people dare to use it; in recording sessions, the red light will easily be turned off and the performer asked to do another "take" because of perceived intonation irregularities.

Enharmonics are another problematic case. In his composition lessons for Thomas Attwood, KV 506a, W. A. Mozart speaks of wide diatonic and small chromatic semitones. Enharmonic shifts on non-keyboard instruments would often have been clearly heard and felt. This applies even (or especially) to enharmonic changes occurring on tied or repeated notes. The pitch drops when c♭² becomes b♮¹, as happens in the third movement of Wilhelm Friedemann Bach's flute duet in E♭ major (Falck 55). In measures 45–49, the second flute plays c♭² a number of times, which is changed into b-natural¹ at the end of measure 49. Quantz points to this problematic spot in his *Solfeggi,* a manuscript collection of short commented excerpts presumably assembled for or by a student (the preface of the current modern edition is quite incorrect in stating that the only extant copy of these *Solfeggi* was actually penned by Quantz himself.) In measure 45, he writes about the c♭²: "rein, etwas auswärts gedreht" (pure, turned out somewhat—in order to play sharper). Again in measure 49, he writes: "so viel just als vorher auswärts" (turned out just as much as before). There is no comment to the b♮¹, which thus should be played in the standard embouchure position, and not turned out, thus lower than the c♭². There are some unusual situations, such as Mozart's symphony KV 543, where we find a "fifth" a♭—d♯¹ and an "octave" a♭¹—g♯². Here the instruments with the flats end their motif at the same moment as those with sharps start their motif. I would surmise that fifths, unisons, and octaves are kept pure, as probably is done in the piano concerto KV 595, where the piano plays a sustained d♭¹ against c♯¹ in the bassoon. I do not believe that any general rule can or should be made; the possibilities (and impossibilities) and the desired expression will direct my choices.

Even in less complicated matters than enharmonic shifts, not all performers will have the same tuning preferences. This is how I usually proceed in ensembles. When there is a keyboard instrument, bass players should stay in unison with the keyboard temperament—they often sit next to it and thus could not easily adopt a different tuning—whereas the other instruments play pure intervals on the bass note, as far as possible. Consequently they do not play in the keyboard's temperament, unless an unavoidable and audible unison would occur. Generally, the fewer instruments playing next to the keyboard, the more they might have to follow its temperament. In smaller ensembles without keyboard, and if the music does not modulate too far, the string players can tune the open strings that lie in the tonic and dominant chords of the piece in pure fifths, and compensate by making smaller fifths elsewhere. But even with equally tempered fifths, there is no need to play everything in equal temperament. In the orchestra, and particularly in classical music where the winds hold long chords, it is essential that on the important chords the winds play pure intervals on the given bass note. Thus they will reinforce each other's overtones, and create a very strongly resonating harmonic background, even when the open strings are tuned slightly differently. A slight difference in tuning between harmony and melody can be less disturbing than a long out-of-tune chord.

Melody playing can also gain by using pure intervals, for example in the performance of duets for two high instruments, where the *difference tone* can reinforce their resonance or even create a perfect bass line. When the sequence g^2-a^2-g^2 is played simultaneously with c^2-f^2-e^2, a "virtual" bass line c^1-f-c is heard. Indeed, when two relatively high notes are sounded together, a humming lower sound can clearly be perceived, at the difference of their respective frequencies. Thus a pure fifth c^2-g^2 will yield a pure c^1, a pure third f^2-a^2 produces a pure f, and so forth. These bass notes can be used as a touchstone for pure tuning, since slight impurities in the played interval produce much greater deviations in the pitch of the difference tone.

In practice, knowing what is historically "correct" is not enough; good ears, a quick realization of each note's function within the given harmony, and a willingness to experiment and adapt will help us to find the best compromise.

Tempo, rhythm, phrasing, articulation, dynamics, sound ideal, and orna-
mentation frequently interact with one another. Taken together, I see them
as ingredients of the performer's "practical" rhetoric. Rhetoric in music and
in language are naturally related; in both fields they help communicate the
message to the audience in a convincing way. From the vantage point of the
author or composer, rhetoric enables the artful expressing and ordering of
their ideas, so that the form enhances the content, both on the structural
and emotional level. I would define the performer's rhetoric as the efficient
transmission of the text (literary and/or musical) to the listener, making
the audience both understand and feel its meaning, simultaneously commu-
nicating on many different levels. Though music and language are related,
"music starts where words end," as the proverb goes. Consequently, we
cannot expect musical rhetoric to be identical to language-based rhetoric.
However, since speaking about music is difficult, and because language-
based rhetoric is a convenient tool for analyzing literary texts, for many
centuries scholars have been tempted to use language-based rhetoric as
a valid system for speaking about music as well. It is my opinion that this
might function to some extent, but it can also lead us away from purely mu-
sical matters. (Why should we construct or want to analyze a sonata move-
ment in the same way as a public speech?) The application of language-
based rhetoric to music can feel like using a wrong unit of measurement,
like trying to measure a building in hertz or decibels. I would rather look
at the individual characteristics of performing arts: poets, actors, dancers,
conductors, singers, and instrumentalists all have their own sets of rules
and conventions, which are accepted and recognized by their audiences.
Evidently, these rules vary over time.

3. TEMPO AND RUBATO

Many details about tempo and rubato can be found in Klaus Mieh-ling, *Das Tempo in der Musik von Barock und Vorklassik* (1993), Clive Brown, *Classical and Romantic Performance Practice, 1750–1900* (1999), and Richard Hudson, *Stolen Time: The History of Tempo Rubato* (1994).

There are few precise descriptions of tempo before the metronome came into general use during the nineteenth century. Even then, they are not necessarily to be taken at face value; recordings (from ca. 1900 onward) show that composers such as Alexander Scriabin and Edward Elgar frequently performed their own pieces at another tempo than the one they prescribe. We know the duration of some pieces, but this might be approximate as well, and it is not always evident which of the repeats were played. Some authors, such as Étienne Loulié and Michel l'Affilard, described (rather than prescribed) tempo by means of a pendulum, from where we can calculate metronome markings. In his *Versuch*, Quantz expresses his tempo prescriptions in simple proportions of an average human heartbeat of 80 beats per minute: 160, 120, 80, and 40. Though he accepts that there can be small deviations, he considers his system as generally valid for instrumental music. In reality, the practice may well have been very much more varied. For example, in Quantz's own works, I found sixteen qualifiers attached to *Allegro*. They are: *di molto, non molto, assai, più tosto assai, con brio, fiero, scherzando, con spirito, spirituoso, ma non troppo, ma non tanto, ma non presto, poco, moderato, grazioso, gustoso.* Even if these qualifiers mainly describe the general character of the movement, they will certainly also affect its tempo.

Their students or contemporaries gave some precise tempo indications for works by Haydn, Mozart, or Beethoven. I regret that so few of these, or nineteenth-century metronome marks, are taken seriously, even by Early Music specialists.

Sometimes we find relative values—today we are taught that *Vivace* is faster than *Allegro,* but Telemann (in the preface to *Harmonische Gottes-Dienst,* 1725) wanted it slower. This does not necessarily apply to all of Telemann's contemporaries, but for his own works, or at least for this cantata collection, it is useful information. Neither do all indications need to mean the same thing in different countries, nor in translation. Studying the notation and the number of short note values written, an Italian *Allegro* often had a faster pulse than a French *Gayment,* though both words basically have the same meaning. Tempi were often related to dances, but even there we meet with different traditions: a minuet or a gavotte was not danced at the same speed everywhere and at all times. When a dance is no longer danced but rather exists as an independent instrumental piece, it can become more sophisticated and complicated, and thus would be performed more slowly. Conversely, W. A. Mozart's letter from Bologna to his sister (March 24, 1770) speaks of the slow danced minuet tempo in Milan, as opposed to the faster symphonic tempo in Austria. Nevertheless, we would expect to recognize the basic character of a given dance, mostly due to its fundamental rhythmic shape. In today's Early Music practice, regrettably, much historical information about dance tempi does not find its way onto the stage.

Even if we do not know the absolute tempi, the proportion of tempo between two sections of a piece can be indicated by the time signatures. In the French ouverture, as established by Lully, the beginning is most often notated in 2 or ¢. The difference between these time signatures is not always clear. Georg Muffat, in the introduction to his *Florilegium Primum* (1695), wants 2 to be slower than ¢, and cites his teacher, Lully, as providing evidence for this. Hotteterre, who was trained in the same Lullian tradition, says the opposite in the very extensive and interesting section on time signatures of his *L'Art de Préluder* (1719). However, he adds that Lully himself did not always distinguish between the two. The following *fugato* section is usually written in 3, with the half bar of the first 2 or ¢ section corresponding to the whole bar of the second. As a general rule this is certainly useful, but quite often, qualifiers or deviating time signatures such as $\frac{3}{8}$ instead of $\frac{3}{4}$ or 3 indicate that the ratio can be variable. In numerous pieces (sticking to flute repertoire: J. S. Bach's second Orchestral Suite BWV 1067, the *Solo pour la flute traversière* BWV 1013, or the B-minor sonata BWV 1030), strict observance of simple mathematical proportions between sections or movements makes one or the other tempo sound unconvincing or impossible to play.

In many situations, the character rather than the tempo might be indicated; I understand *Vivace* as a prescription to play lively, in whatever tempo. Telemann's *Vivace* movements will often have more diverse rhythmic values and patterns (in a mixture of eighth, sixteenth, and thirty-second notes) than his *Allegros*, which mostly include only eighth and sixteenth notes. Thus, though the tempo will be somewhat slower, in the *Vivace* we will hear a greater liveliness through additional variety and through the faster speed of the shortest notes than in the *Allegro*. Character differences can be very subtle: I would not consider *Gavotte gaye*; *Gavotte, gay*; and *Gavotte, gayment* as entirely synonymous. In the first, the character is given by the piece itself, whereas in the last the performer is more responsible for it. The second seems less specified and might lie in the middle. In practice, I often observe a gradation from the most overtly gay in the first case (no pun intended), to a more gentle character in the last.

The environment in which the music is played always has its influence on the tempo, so that for the same piece, different tempi might have been thought appropriate in different situations. The determining external factors are the varying acoustics, size, and particular venue (opera, ballroom, music room in a palace, private home, church, or open air); the choice of instrument (the harpsichord may permit a faster tempo than the organ); the size of an ensemble; character and capacity of players; the presence or absence of an audience; the nature and size of the audience; and the audience's musical taste and education. Nevertheless, we read of individual performers' tendencies. Though this is doubtlessly interesting, it is also relative, as we do not know to which standards it relates. Some examples: J. S. Bach is reputed to have played fast; performers of the Berlin school in the second half of the eighteenth century took *Allegros* very fast and *Adagios* very slow (this had immediate influence on ornamentation, as we shall see later); Franz Schubert is said to have observed tempo very strictly.

How regular was the tempo intended to be? In recitatives, the singer had to follow the character and rhythm of the words. Whereas in France this was quite precisely indicated through frequent changes of time signature, in Italian, English, and German compositions the singer had to find out for himself how to handle this element, aiming at a forceful declamation of the literary text. For other genres, treatises often stress steadiness of tempo, but that could be merely pedagogical. In music for the dance one can suppose that a steady rhythm is essential, but is this rigidity still essential once a dance has become an independent instrumental or vocal piece? In his very detailed singing treatise *Remarques curieuses sur l'art de bien chanter* (1668), Bénigne de Bacilly says that some gavottes are sung in free tempo, as airs, whereas in other pieces one has to observe the exact proportions of meter, as in dance music. When François Couperin appends the direction *mesuré* to some pieces, does this mean that all his other works were to be performed freely—and if so, how freely?

Authors such as Roger North, Pier F. Tosi, C. P. E. Bach, W. A. Mozart, and F. Chopin most often describe rubato as the free playing of a solo part against strictly observed tempo in the accompaniment. I call this the "old" rubato, as opposed to the "modern" rubato where all parts change tempo. Since it is very seldom explicitly asked for in the score, knowing where, when and how to apply the "old" of rubato belongs to a soloist's training and good taste. I hypothesize that this kind of rubato could be meant in some passages that are notated in syncopations, with the bass on the beats, and the melody in between, as occurs quite frequently in Pietro Locatelli, C. P. E. Bach, and W. A. Mozart. This form of rubato was obviously considered exquisite, but difficult to perform. Today, it is rarely heard. I can only dream of a pianist playing a beautiful passage in a slow movement of a Mozart sonata with rubato in the right hand against the steady left hand, as Mozart himself describes it in his letter of October 24, 1777, to his father:

daß ich immer accurat im tact bleybe, über das verwundern sie sich alle. Das Tempo rubato in einem Adagio, daß die lincke hand nichts darum weiß, können sie gar nicht begreifen, bey ihnen giebt die lincke hand nach. (Everybody is astonished that I always stay accurately in tempo. They cannot understand the *tempo rubato* in an *Adagio,* when the left hand ignores what the right does; with them, the left hand follows the right hand.)

The second movement of Mozart's sonata for harpsichord with accompanying violin, KV 7 (1764), shows us that Mozart must have already acquired this skill at very young age (see figure 1).

Figure 1. W. A. Mozart, *Adagio* from Sonata for Keyboard and Violin, KV 7 (1764), mm. 1–6.

When the accompaniment follows the rubato of the melody, the basic tempo is lost and the "modern" rubato takes the place of the old; this adds a totally different stylistic flavor to the music. In his *Versuch über die wahre Art das Clavier zu spielen* (1753 and 1762, with additions in 1787), C. P. E. Bach speaks of the modern rubato as well, but he recommends its use only by a soloist or by a small and well-rehearsed ensemble. He suggests for instance to play more slowly when we repeat a passage in minor instead of major. Significantly, C. P. E. Bach strongly warns against any unconscious use of it.

Both forms of rubato existed side by side into the twentieth century, but the subtler "one against the others" variety was gradually superseded by the more obvious general tempo change. Richard Wagner, who maintained that each bar must have its own tempo, exemplified the tempo change type. Claude Debussy appears to have disagreed. In the latter's compositions, we can find within the same piece (see his sonata for flute, viola, and harp or *Syrinx*) frequent indications of tempo changes (stepwise or gradual *accelerando* or *ritardando*), but also *rubato*. I can only suppose that in this case the basic tempo remains unchanged.

The use of both kinds of rubato varied a lot from one place or time to another and from one musician to another. Italian violinists of the eighteenth century were reputed to play quite freely; Charles Burney, who gives us so much valuable insider information in his travel diaries, tells us that when Francesco Geminiani was the leader at the Naples opera, his rubato and frequent tempo changes created chaos around him, and Quantz vividly describes how Italian violinists could ruin the orchestra's cohesion. As is so often the case in writings about music, we cannot know how far the performers went, what was tolerable and what was not, and for whom. Consequently, in today's historically informed performance practice, and not only with respect to rubato, the question to be asked is, should we try to follow the "good" or the "bad" example? And good or bad according to whose taste? Do we want a historically correct orchestra, playing out of tune and not together, only because it has been described that such orchestras existed? Or was this chaos part of the excitement and fire that were frequently associated with Italian music, and are we robbing this music of one of its essential qualities, by over-polishing it, when we try to avoid such excesses (at least, excesses for our modern ears)? I can only suggest that we experiment, with historical knowledge and courage. Sticking to received tradition might feel safer to the performers and will likely not disturb their audiences, but it feels like a missed opportunity.

4. RHYTHM

Stephen E. Hefling has written the most complete study of inequality and related matters: *Rhythmic Alteration in Seventeenth- and Eighteenth-Century Music* (1993). Occasionally, however, I would interpret some historic texts differently or establish connections to the spoken word more strongly. In the November 2007 and February 2012 issues of *Early Music,* John Byrt gives very interesting examples of inequality in Italian-style compositions from the end of the seventeenth and first half of the eighteenth centuries.

The eighteenth-century musician did not observe our modern rules about strict solfège down to the smallest note values. These notes seemed to be treated as ornamental rather than essential, and could thus be performed more freely, some longer, some shorter than notated. The next higher rhythmic unit, however, would remain unaffected by these changes.

One can easily link this inequality of the shortest note values to the iambic (short-long) or trochaic (long-short) verse feet, which were, at least since Greek and Roman antiquity, in general use in poetry and theatre all over Europe. Whereas in today's colloquial speech the implied rhythmic inequality is mostly neglected, this was not (yet) the case in the seventeenth and eighteenth century's theatrical declamation, or in singing. A typical example is Gluck's famous *Che faro senza Euridice* (from *Orfeo ed Euridice*, 1762), or *J'ai perdu mon Euridice* in the French version (1774). The singer's first two notes were written as equal eighth notes, but even today most people (justly) sing the first note much longer than the second, as necessitated by correct metrical diction. Interestingly, in his remarks about the Cramer piano etudes, Beethoven is still speaking about the verse feet, requiring exact knowledge and application of them; very consequently, he recommends rhythmic inequality of the shortest notes in some of these etudes, which he saw as the best preparation for his own piano compositions. I would love to hear this approach, at least sometime.

In German, the accented syllable or note is expressed more (but not exclusively) by strength than by length. We find this clearly illustrated in Johann Gottfried Walther's *Praecepta der musikalischen Composition* (1707) and in his *Musicalisches Lexicon* (1732); he uses the phrase "meine Seele ruft und schreyet" to demonstrate the alternating long and short syllables, which he calls "innerlich lang" or "innerlich kurz," but "äusserlich gleich" (intrinsically long or intrinsically short, but externally—in their written form—identical). According to him, they should be sung or played as strong and weak, respectively, and the weak note should also be somewhat shorter. In French declamation, the stress is given by length rather than by strength; the accented syllable is pronounced approximately twice as long as the unaccented syllable. The actual degree of inequality would depend on the text to be recited or sung. Indeed, the *a* in *amour* must be made less long than the *plai* in *plaisir,* as Bénigne de Bacilly explains in the very lengthy chapter about pronunciation and prosody in his *Remarques curieuses sur l'art de bien chanter* (1668).

In Italian singing as well, the text can be more easily understood if the metrical structure of the verse is respected. In vocal music on Italian text, especially from the first half of the eighteenth century, we find numerous practical indications of inequality similar to the Gluck example already cited. Composers such as A. Scarlatti, G. Bononcini, or L. Vinci in Italy; G. F. Handel in England; and R. Keiser in Germany frequently write equal sixteenth notes in a vocal part (in syllabic as well as melismatic passages), but use dotted notation when the same motifs are to be performed by the basso continuo, obbligato instruments, or orchestra. Clearly, the singer is supposed to know which syllables must be sung longer or shorter, according to the metric structure of the text, whereas the absence of text necessitates a somewhat more precise notation for the instrumentalists. It is obvious that in Italian, too, the exact degree of inequality will depend on the specific text to be sung.

Instrumentalists were always required to take singers as their model, and indeed they will have needed to listen attentively to the singer in order to imitate or accompany well at appropriate places. In purely instrumental music, they will have applied a similar flexibility or have imagined a text under their notes.

The request for unequal performance of equally written short notes is documented from 1550 until ca. 1800. It is not surprising that we find most (but by no means all) references to this principle in France, where the rhythmic inequality is most inherent in the prosody of the language. The numerous treatises, for instruments as well as for voices, generally agree with one another about the use of the *notes inégales*. Systematically, the note that falls on the beat or on the subdivision thereof is lengthened, and the following note is shortened. The ratio between long and short can change according to character, but seldom reaches the dotted rhythm's ratio of 3:1. In the preface to his *Livre d'orgue* (1665), Guillaume Nivers gives a beautiful description of inequality: "[on rajoute] comme des demi-points" (one adds something like half a dot). Exempted from inequality were very fast notes, triplets and in some situations larger intervals and repeated notes. With respect to this last category, repeated notes, various notations of the *Marseillaise* (1792) are informative. Rouget de Lisle wrote the beginning in dotted rhythm and many other editions do the same, but quite a number of sources of the same time are notated using equal notes. I suppose everybody knew how to sing or play the tune, regardless of the equal notation!

After studying all the sources, it becomes clear that the French *inégalité* is not an ornament, not an option, but is pure necessity. Good taste consisted in knowing *how* unequal one had to sing or play, but not whether or not one would apply inequality. That was a foregone conclusion. In French compositions, inequality is not usually called for verbatim; everybody knew where it occurred, and only in exceptional situations were specific remarks, both prescriptive and prohibitive, required.

Just as the splendor of Versailles was imitated everywhere in Europe, the French music (one of the salient ingredients of Louis XIV's court), and especially the suite form, with its overture and dances, became very popular in Germany and England. Composers such as J. S. Bach, Handel, and Telemann wrote many suites in the French style. Henry Purcell and Handel used it in their operas and keyboard works, and even Archangelo Corelli, Antonio Vivaldi, and Francesco Maria Veracini occasionally adopted it. We do not know how expertly these foreigners played in the French style, with the appropriate ornaments and *notes inégales*. However, since some orchestras counted Lully's students or followers in their ranks or as their leaders, one could expect a fair degree of knowledge and tradition to be passed on. Outside of France, I would thus expect many dances of French origin to have been played with an eloquent inequality. Obviously, the results will have varied; there was no radio, no recording, and no television.

It is less clear whether outside of France inequality was generally adopted for pieces that were *not* written in the French *ouverture* or dance style. Except for Quantz, few German, English, or Italian authors mention inequality very much in their theoretical writings. If it was used at all, it seems to have been less omnipresent than in France. Instead of inequality we frequently encounter the concept of "good" and "bad" notes, the first being stronger, not necessarily also longer than the second (we shall meet this concept again in next sections). Quantz, however, wants us to apply inequality in *all* music (he never mentions inequality especially in connection with French music). He stands quite alone with this request, but as a very influential artist in the mid-eighteenth century, he might have had many followers. It is quite clear where he got this idea. He will have been familiar with the French inequality from his studies with the famous French flautist Buffardin, who was principal flute in what was then the very French-minded Dresden court orchestra, led by Volumier, another Frenchman and possibly a student of Lully's. On the other hand, Quantz had had the occasion to hear the best Italian singers during his travels to Vienna and Italy, and throughout his later professional life in the (then more Italianate) Dresden orchestra and in Berlin. In his treatise, Quantz insists that instrumentalists have to model their performance on the Italian singing tradition, and we have seen that inequality in Italian vocal music was widespread, even if it was mostly not notated and probably less systematical than in France. As Quantz was influenced by French as well as Italian practice of inequality, it comes as no surprise that his rules for the correct application of inequality, as expressed in the *Versuch* (1752), are not identical with the virtually unanimous rules of countless French treatises. Interestingly, inequality appears more than thirty times in Quantz's treatise and thus receives a more detailed and nuanced treatment than his simple and often-quoted basic rules would suggest. Many additional examples and exceptions are found in Quantz's above-mentioned *Solfeggi*. These can be understood as nuances or exceptions to the general rules, because the application of inequality at these very spots might not have been totally evident for everybody. We thus receive invaluable firsthand information about specific passages from well-known flute compositions by Quantz himself, Telemann, W. F. Bach, and other colleagues and friends. I cannot quite understand why so many players continue to ignore this instruction.

Inequality in Italian music is also well documented in France. Some want to believe that this only shows the peculiar French habit of performing everything "à la Française," but a number of indications convince me that in this case, the inequality is factually based on Italian examples. Hotteterre le Romain (presumably so called because he had worked in Rome, from 1698 to 1700, during the days of Corelli's greatest fame) quoted many Corelli examples in a lengthy explanation about time signatures and their effect upon inequality in *L'Art de Préluder* (1719). He is an important ear-witness to Corelli's playing, and it seems very strange that he would choose to quote Corelli for inequality if he had heard him play these very pieces equally. The picture emerging from Michel Corrette's treatises for violin (1738 and ca. 1782), violoncello (1741), flute (ca. 1742), and pardessus de viole (1748) seems to indicate that whereas he wants the eighth notes in Italian music performed equally, the sixteenth must generally be played unequally. In the flute method, for example, he writes that in Italian *Allegro* or *Presto* sonata or concerto movements in C or ₵, one *sometimes* (my italics) plays equal sixteenth notes. In those years in Paris,

Corrette must have heard numerous Italian musicians in the *Concerts Spirituels* and elsewhere. Just as for Hotteterre, it feels strange that he would prescribe another practice than the one he himself had heard.

Regrettably, the uncertainty surrounding the application of inequality (where and how much) seems to lead many performers away from it, even in French music. Johann Mattheson compares this in his *Kern melodischer Wissenschaft* (1737) and again in *Der vollkommene Kapellmeister* (1739) to cooking without salt.

Another frequent deviation from the rhythmic notation is overdotting. This can be, but does not need to be, a consequence of inequality; if the eighth notes must be played unequally, the eighth note after a dotted quarter will be shortened as well. However, over-dotting exists independently of inequality: many German sources from the second half of the eighteenth century request us to lengthen the dot and perform the note(s) after the dot as late and fast as possible, from dotted eighth notes downward, but from dotted quarters in *alla breve* time. This "double dot" must not necessarily be entirely played; there could also be a silence instead of the dot(s). The over-dotting principle is not limited to French *ouvertures,* where it is especially effective. According to Quantz, C. P. E. Bach, Leopold Mozart and others, over-dotting needs to be generally applied.

On the other hand, under-dotting is mentioned in connection with the simultaneous appearance of dotted rhythms and triplets. Quantz and C. P. E. Bach in their *Versuch,* and J. F. Agricola in an article in the *Allgemeine deutsche Bibliothek* (1769), all working at the same time at the court of Frederick the Great, each formulate quite different solutions to this problem. Quantz wants the dotted rhythm to be overdotted, thus the note after the dot to be performed as late as possible after the third note of the triplet. C. P. E. Bach wants the note after the dot simultaneous with the last note of the triplet (under-dotting). Otherwise he finds the effect disagreeable, and the execution difficult. Agricola has the most flexible and practical approach and lets it depend on tempo; he prescribes that only in a very fast tempo, the note after the dot is played simultaneously with the last note of the triplet. He cites his revered teacher J. S. Bach as his authority, but of course J. S. Bach was also C. P. E. Bach's only teacher, as C. P. E. proudly states, and Agricola was also a student of C. P. E. Bach and Quantz. Adapting dotted rhythm to simultaneous triplets can be found in actual notation at least until Schubert and Chopin.

I have frequently met another situation where under-dotting could be called for, though I have never found any direct mention of it. The top part of many opening slow or moderately slow movements of Italian, English, or German sonatas of the first half of the eighteenth century (by Handel, among others) consists of almost continuous pairs of a dotted sixteenth note and a thirty-second note. These movements are not in *ouverture* style and the normal over-dotting makes them very stiff and stern. The clue for under-dotting them can be found in France, where F. Couperin states in *L'Art de toucher le Clavecin* (1717) that non-French composers generally notated the rhythm they wanted to hear, in contrast to the French composers' convention of implied but not notated inequality. However, French inequality is too subtle and varied to be precisely written down, but definitely did not sound equal. Couperin might thus have notated these very passages with equal notes, knowing that they would be performed unequally anyway. Outside France, performers needed to be told to do so. Consequently a non-French composer wanting to hear something like inequality had no other choice than to write the closest approximation: dotted notes. Indeed, I have never seen a non-French score requesting "inequality *à la française,* please." Since inequality itself is normally less than dotted, this Italian-English-German equivalent might require under- rather than over-dotting as well. The variable proportion between the long and the short note, as in French *inégalité,* makes these movements much more flexible and expressive. I suppose that their unequal performance will have sounded quite similar to the inequality encountered in Italian-style vocal music, as explained above.

On the whole it becomes obvious that the rhythmic interpretation of seventeenth- and eighteenth-century music, at least in the shorter note values, was not slavish. We have a choice, and thus we must choose, with knowledge and a sense of responsibility. Playing the notation literally is not always an adequate option, unless we definitely choose, for some reason, to do exactly that.

Figure 2. F. Geminiani, *Esempio XX* from *The Art of Playing on the Violin*, op. IX (1751, here unaltered from second edition, Bremner, London ca. 1765, p. 27). With kind permission of the Library of the Brussels Royal Conservatory (B-Bc 8905).

In Geminiani's highly interesting *The Art of Playing on the Violin* (1751), several different ways of playing some standard passages are shown, both in fast and slow tempi. The most literal and straightforward interpretations—which are those we hear most frequently today—Geminiani calls "mediocre," "cattivo" (bad), "pessimo" (very bad), or "cattivo o particolare" (in most cases it is bad, but as a special effect it can be good) (see figure 2).

One could ask why composers did not write more precisely. They presumably did not need to, since performers would know what to do, or it did not matter so much: good taste can have many different shades, indeed.

Whereas tempo and rhythm are at least approximately given by the composer, phrasing, articulation, and dynamics (the basic elements of the performer's "elocutio") were often not indicated at all. Two brilliant recent studies, the first about the sixteenth century, the second about the eighteenth century, elaborate this wide field. They do not start from anachronistic and/or fashionable concepts, but through diligent and in-depth reading of contemporary documents, compositions and treatises about solmisation, counterpoint, fugue, composition, keyboard, basso continuo, and rhetoric yield fascinating "views from within" upon the relative performance practice conventions regarding expression, phrasing, dynamics, etc. I thank both authors for generously having shared their ideas with me during their work:

Anne Smith. The Performance of 16th-Century Music: Learning from
   the Theorists *(2011).*

Ewald Demeyere. Johann Sebastian Bach's *Art of Fugue,* Performance
   Practice Based on German Eighteenth-Century Theory *(publication forthcoming in 2013).*

5. PHRASING

In most of today's mainstream musical performances we hear "long-line playing": the horizontal aspect clearly dominates, and sometimes almost annihilates, the vertical aspect. Each note is quite similar to its neighbors to the left and right, and changes are made very gradually. In earlier times, music, just as society, was not so democratic; not all notes were equal. We have already seen that not all twelve semitones were equal, that shorter notes can be performed with inequality, and now we will see that the hierarchical principle extends much further.

When we compare music and language, we can equate the grammatical phrase with the musical phrase: it is the expression of a more or less complex meaningful entity. Musical phrasing can then be understood as the intelligible rendering of that meaningful entity, as pertaining to the emotional and structural contents of the phrase. Our Flemish word for phrase or sentence is *zin*. This is obviously related to the English word sense, but it has even more interesting meanings and connotations. It can also mean direction, goal, purpose, significance, desire, or pleasure. As well, *zin* is used to indicate the five senses, and is linked to sensibility, sensitivity, sensuality, and so forth. In my opinion, a textual or musical phrase that does not include most of these aspects "makes no sense."

In long-line playing, the *zin* (in all meanings) and the declamation of individual words are sacrificed to the continuous streaming of the sound, to the horizontal line. Herbert von Karajan's recordings might have been the culmination of this style (his same *Berlin Philharmonic Orchestra* under Sir Simon Rattle has moved somewhat away from it). In the best case the general affect of the phrase is expressed; in the worst case there is only an outer beauty of sound. Basically it is the consequent application of rules that were already prescribed by Hugo Riemann in his *Musikalische Dynamik und Agogik, Lehrbuch des Phrasierens* (1884) and *System der musikalischen Rhythmik und Metrik* (1903). One could summarize the system as the following:

- Music goes per upbeat.
- You reach the climax by pushing toward it with crescendo and accelerando; after the climax you make diminuendo and ritardando.
- When the melody moves up, you make crescendo and accelerando; when it moves down, you make diminuendo and ritardando. (In the second half of the twentieth century, the accelerando-ritardando element progressively went out of fashion, probably being judged as too romantic.)

Surprisingly enough, many Early Music specialists are heard to follow these very principles, though it can easily be demonstrated that historically they would be the exception rather than the rule. This late-romantic phrasing is of course what we all have grown up with, and it is easily recognizable and understood by a broad and non-specialist audience. It has thus found favor with many performers, even for music that has been composed according to a different set of conventions. This is quite understandable, but in my opinion, the price for easy success is too high; earlier compositions treated in this later style will lose part of their *zin*. The thicker performance sauce all but covers a number of the compositions' characteristics. Monteverdi and Verdi, Rossi and Rossini, Bach and Offenbach then sound all too similar.

As is often the case with theorists, rather than being innovative, Riemann probably systematized what had slowly developed over some generations and had become current practice—not unlike Quantz's attitude, in fact. Which rules do we find before Riemann? Singing treatises often give us very valuable information, since singers were considered to be the ideal performers, who furthermore could rely on the literary text in order to shape and refine their musical phrasing. Instrumental treatises such as those by Quantz, C. P. E. Bach, and L. Mozart always cite good singers as the examples to be imitated. General principles found in these sources include the following:

- A "good note" (this idea will be further explained in the section about dynamics) and stressed syllables or notes will be preceded by a silence rather than being pushed into, or can even come late.

- Poetic feet are judged to be of great importance for composers and performers, as is documented by Mattheson's *Der vollkommene Kapellmeister* (1739) and elsewhere, and is still present in Beethoven's annotations of the Cramer piano etudes.

- Comparable to good prosody, we should use differentiated dynamics within the bar—I would call these "microdynamics" (see section 7). This precludes the general pushing of the notes toward the next climax or toward the last note of the phrase.

In my opinion, these ideas are strongly linked to the bel canto technique from before ca. 1840, which was duly imitated on all instruments. There, great importance was attached to the *sons filés* (a crescendo-diminuendo on one single longer note); further, a raise in pitch did not automatically include a crescendo, but rather a diminuendo. The transition from this vocal ideal into "modern" singing, where equality and homogeneity are stressed and where high notes are generally sung more loudly and heavily, often in disregard of text accent, is clearly illustrated around the middle of the nineteenth century by the famous voice and piano teacher Friedrich Wieck, Schumann's father-in-law. In his ironic but highly interesting *Clavier und Gesang, Didaktisches und Polemisches* (1853), he strongly takes a position against the new fashion. Wieck sees the same tendency in piano playing as in singing, the sacrifice of elegance to force.

6. ARTICULATION

With regard to articulation, singing treatises are of great help, as they stress the singer's obligation to clearly pronounce consonants as well as vowels and to respect the correct prosody. The fact that this is stressed so often probably indicates that in earlier times, too, not all singers fulfilled this obligation. Goethe was not all that flattering, when he said in 1807: "Vokalmusik heißt sie, weil man beim (jetzigen) Singen nur die Vokalen hört!" ("One speaks of vocal music because nowadays with singers one only hears the vowels"—the pun does not work as well in English.)

Also in matters of articulation, we can compare music to language; we should not only speak correctly but also understand the difference between colloquial speech and public declamation. I am convinced that the invention of the microphone and loudspeaker has had a disastrous effect on declamation and rhetoric. Radio or TV newsreaders have learned to speak clearly and quietly into the microphone, without emotional accents. For example, "two thousand people killed in an earthquake" and "generally, clear skies are expected today" are said similarly. This kind of neutral "public" voice (though it is actually recorded alone in a studio) has become all too familiar. It threatens to become the model, not only for public speaking but also for playing. Everything sounds nice, clear, clean, and even; there are no risks and no problems. The danger is that we might start to feel the same as our voices sound, insensitive to the emotional contents of the message.

Another consequence of microphones and loudspeakers is that teachers, lawyers, priests, popular singers, and even actors are no longer required to develop their voices to resonate and project; technology will do the job for them. Listening to old recordings of the Comédie Francaise, of de Gaulle, Hitler (ignoring the content), Churchill, or Dr. Martin Luther King Jr. (his "I Have a Dream" speech of 1963), we hear variable tempo and rhythm, great inflections of pitch and dynamics, and ample vibrato on words that should inspire passion. The famous early-twentieth-century Viennese actor Alexander Moissi (1879–1935) eminently displayed the same characteristics, maybe more than anybody else. His recordings of, for example, Goethe's *Erlkönig* or *Faust,* or Shakespeare's *Hamlet,* make us understand that Schoenberg's "Sprechgesang" in *Pierrot Lunaire* (1912) is basically the writing down of what actors were already doing, only connecting it, rather vaguely, to pitch and time. Grétry writes in his *Mémoires ou Essays sur la Musique* (1789–1797) that hearing actors recite their text greatly facilitated his composition of vocal music; the recitation gave him melody and rhythm (see section 4 for the metric recitation). Today, we might accuse this kind of declamation of being exaggerated or unnatural—whatever that is. On the other hand, I am not sure that modern actors would necessarily be good models for composers.

As in phrasing, instrumentalists should also imitate singers in terms of articulation. Again we notice important differences between the modern articulation style and the principles set forth in many old treatises. In the modern style, most notes are played as long as possible, and often every effort is made to have all notes start similarly. This is clearly demonstrated in the quasi-uniform articulation, in legato as in perlé, of so many pianists. Wind and string playing frequently follow the same approach, avoiding audible starts of notes (the equivalent of consonants before the vowels). The famous singer Elisabeth Schwarzkopf, in her book *On and Off the Record* (1982), reveals an interesting fact about this style when speaking of her husband Walter Legge, who was one of the most influential mid-twentieth-century recording directors. She quotes Legge as describing the string sound ideal he himself and Herbert von Karajan developed, as

> exquisitely polished, free of anything that is unbeautiful, of great brilliance, and fortissimo without the click of an attack. . . . We worked together for years on the theory that no entrance must start without

the string vibrating and the bow already moving, and when you get a
moving bow touching an already vibrating string, you get a beautiful
entry. But if either of those bodies is not alive and already moving,
you get a click.

Listening to Karajan's recordings, we notice that he largely reached
his goal and set a new standard; this style became the general model of
most mainstream string playing for the rest of the century, no matter
what era the repertoire.

Seventeenth- and eighteenth-century instruction books, on the
contrary, demand a much more differentiated application of the technical aspects of articulation, such as fingering for keyboards, bowing
for strings, and tonguing for winds. Interestingly, not only the beginning but also the end of the note is discussed in detail. Mainly in faster
tempi, notes were seldom held for their complete value, except when
slurred or when tenuto is explicitly specified. The amount of time individual notes are held also determines their relative weight within the
bar or passage, and thus relates to dynamics. Some general principles:

- Ornaments consisting of many notes (the equivalent of
  coloraturas for the voice) are slurred; otherwise, long slurs are
  rare, though they become increasingly more frequent toward
  the end of the eighteenth century.
- Slurs usually lie within one harmony and are not extended
  over a barline; generally slurs do not connect a weak to a
  strong beat or subdivision thereof.
- Most slurs are expected to produce a diminuendo, and the
  last note under the slur is generally shortened; thus the
  note after the slur is clearly detached (Brahms, in his 1879
  correspondence with his friend the famous violinist Joseph
  Joachim, calls this a generally appropriate refinement in
  performance). Compare this to the modern pianist's habit
  of extending the slur into the first note of the next beat
  or measure, a practice that appears to develop during the
  nineteenth century.
- Notes before appoggiaturas are shortened, in order to give
  more declamatory value to the appoggiatura.

- The less important a note is, the shorter it is held.
- Articulation is proportionate to the size of the intervals to be played: the greater the interval, the shorter the articulation.

The absence of articulation markings in a composition basically means that the performer had to follow the conventional rules of the time and place—as is so often true, "absence of proof does not mean proof of absence." The composer was expected to notate any exceptions to these rules because even a well-trained musician could not necessarily guess where to go against the conventions. Often, music for string instruments had most annotations, since the articulations directed the bowing. String treatises stressed the basic rule that the "good" beats are to be played down-bow much more systematically than is done in modern playing.

Unfortunately articulation does not fare much better than phrasing in much of today's Early Music playing and singing. It is often careless and undifferentiated, and lacks concern for proper declamation. In vocal music, the balance between phrasing and articulation makes a text not only literally understood, but also felt (i.e., understood at an emotional level). It is so rewarding—and all too exceptional—to hear an opera singer whose words can actually be understood without the use of subtitles or supertitles; then, the poetry, music, acting, and decor can collaborate and reinforce one another. However, whereas an attentive and creative listener can more or less easily imagine the latter two, the absence of an understandable text takes away an essential element. In instrumental music, a lack of phrasing and/or articulation provokes much the same effect as in singing. The attention is then drawn to the instrument as an abstract, speechless, beautiful voice, rather than to what is expressed through this sound. As an instrumentalist, I have always been impressed by and jealous of the expressive possibilities of the voice. When this potential is not fully used, I feel strongly disappointed. I can admire a splendid vocal or instrumental sound and a virtuoso technique, but cannot stand them when they seem to become the purpose instead of the means. I compare the voice or instrument to a pencil; what I write with it is more important than the pencil itself, even if it is a golden pencil.

7. DYNAMICS

The description of vocal ideals in this and other sections relies on historical vocal treatises themselves and on modern writings such as John Potter's "Reconstructing Lost Voices," published in Tess Knighton and David Fallows (eds.), *Companion to Medieval & Renaissance Music* (1997); the same author's "The Tenor-Castrato Connection, 1760–1860," published in *Early Music* (February 2007), and the chapters on singing in Howard Mayer Brown and Stanley Sadie (eds.), *Performance Practice: Music after 1600* (1989).

Though dynamics are a very personal element of performance, in Early Music where they are mostly not specified, historical documents such as treatises and descriptions of performances, the instruments themselves, and concert venue acoustics must provide much of our information.

Clearly differentiated micro-dynamics, valid for one note or for a very small group of notes, were predominant. A central concept is the contrast between "good" and "bad" notes within a bar. Good notes are first of all those that fall on the strong beats (1 and 3 in C, 1 in $\frac{2}{4}$ and $\frac{3}{4}$, etc.). This principle is extended down the hierarchical ladder: the first subdivision of a quarter note is better than the second, and the first sixteenth note is better than the second, and so forth. In this manner, a group of four articulated "equal" notes will be played 1 2 3 4, and also longer series of sixteenth notes are not to be performed with equal strength, but the bad ones will be played softer and/or shorter than the good ones. Shorter can mean (1) later, as in *inégalité* (see section 4 about rhythm) or (2) held less long (see section 6 about articulation). Obviously, in vocal music, this makes us stay very close to the prosody of the text and the poetic feet. Vocalizes are, in principle, only allowed on strong syllables.

They normally make a diminuendo, because the impact of the syllable or word lies at the beginning of the vocalize. For instruments, a slur is the equivalent of a vocalize, and thus makes a diminuendo as well (this combines very well with Brahms's request to shorten the last note under a slur, as we have seen in the previous section).

Several elements can change this standard "grid" of dynamics related to the note's position within the bar. Intervals are one factor; they can be compared to the rise or fall of a voice according to its varying degrees of excitement. Harmony is another consideration; dissonances are played stronger than their resolutions (which are normally slurred to the preceding dissonance). In the Quantz *Versuch*, we find dissonances themselves divided into different classes of harshness and, thus, of loudness. Intervals and dissonances can nuance or even overrule the importance of the strong/weak metric position within the bar. However, this will not turn a bad note into a good note; it only makes an accented bad note highly efficient because it is then perceived as exceptional.

As has already been mentioned, the vocal ideal in earlier centuries was very different from modern singing, and instrumentalists were expected to behave like good singers. The voice had a pyramid, not a column character: stronger and broader in the low register and more refined as the sound climbed up. It is only in the 1830s that the tenor's famous high c^2 in Rossini's *Guillaume Tell* was sung in chest voice—and was strongly disliked by Rossini himself. The voice registers needed to be well joined, but difference in register was exploited (Mozart masterfully used this device in his vocal works and concerti). In vocal as well as instrumental tone production, vibrato was not considered to be an inseparable part of the sound as it is now, but an ornament, to be applied with fine judgment, and not too often. The *messa di voce* or *son filé*, the gradual crescendo and diminuendo on one note, was the basic dynamic exercise of any singer, and thus of any good melody-instrument player. Interestingly, Tartini, in his *Traité des Agréments* (before 1756), requires the long notes performed with *messa di voce* to be played absolutely without vibrato. This practice can still be heard on some historical recordings of singers such as Adelina Patti or

Luisa Tetrazzini. Whereas the diminuendo is natural (all sounds eventually die out, just as we do), we can consider the crescendo as "against nature," as life in reverse order, creating awe and tension. Keeping long notes straight is described in Leopold Mozart's *Versuch einer gründlichen Violinschule* (1756) as a special exercise, an afterthought after several bowing exercises with changing dynamics. He considers it useful for mastering the bow, but not as a performance option. On the contrary, he states that each note, even the loudest, must start and finish softly (however brief that softer beginning may be); otherwise it would be an incomprehensible noise. The Klingler Quartet, continuing the tradition of Joseph Joachim, still adhered to this principle, as demonstrated in their recordings from the first third of the previous century.

An interesting field of research, still insufficiently explored, is inquiry into the many volumes of manuscript or printed solfeggi for singers. Among many others, we have highly virtuosic examples by Leonardo Leo, Hasse (for his wife, Faustina, one of the greatest mezzo-sopranos of the eighteenth century), Mozart, and Crescentini. Crescentini's (published in Paris ca. 1820) include very detailed dynamics, which were, in his own words "essential to bringing out musical syntax." These exercises, together with vocal treatises and descriptions of singers' performances, give us a rich picture of vocal aesthetics in the seventeenth through the early nineteenth century. They show a style of performance drastically different from what is common today, even among specialized performers. We can only dream of hearing this style again, and hope that someday a gifted young singer dares to move in that direction, without too much readiness for compromise. The difference between early and modern singing is not only that there are no castrati anymore!

There is a still ongoing development toward louder and more homogenous instruments and voices, as concert venues and orchestras grow in size. Antonio Bagatella, a violin maker associated with Tartini, wrote an important treatise on violin making, *Regole per la costruzione de' violini viole violoncelli e violoni* (written in 1782 and published in 1786). He expresses the view that two sound ideals exist for the violin: the round and soft "voce umana" for solo playing and the more penetrating "voce argentina" for orchestral playing. W. A. Mozart recognizes this difference in a letter to his father (October 6, 1777). The *Buttergeige,* which the four- or five-year-old Wolfgang loved so much, as testified by Johann Andreas Schachtner's letter to Mozart's sister (April 24, 1792), presumably belonged to the former category. Around 1800 or somewhat later, this idea was abandoned; solo instruments had to become louder. The same motivation of greater volume and evenness is the reason for technological "improvements" in other instruments. During the last decades of the eighteenth century, woodwinds were equipped with an increasing number of chromatic keys, keys or valves were developed for brass instruments, and keyboard instruments were designed with a longer sound and a slower diminuendo. Comparing the modern Steinway with a Cristofori piano, the player feels invited to consider his use of dynamics afresh and to include many micro-dynamic shadings on the earlier instrument.

Evolution with its construct of adaptation for survival is not necessarily synonymous with overall improvement; instruments may gain in evenness and volume—but might at the same time lose variety of colors and delicacy. The tendency of favoring force over finesse, very noticeable in Early Music as well as in "standard" performances, has been compared to the inflation of superlatives in today's spoken language. This was what Maurice Raskin, the well-known Belgian violin virtuoso and pedagogue told me in the early 1970s. He added that in his youth, during the 1920s and 1930s, violinists never played as loudly as they did fifty years later.

When micro-dynamics are omnipresent—mostly not notated but very systematically codified and observed—macro-dynamics, extending over longer passages, cannot be very important. They would indeed render the smaller effects insignificant, go against all conventions, and make everything equal, as is the case in the twentieth century's long-line playing. We find macro-dynamics notated in a few typical situations: (1) as an echo effect or (2) as an indication of tutti and solo episodes in a concerto or aria. In these cases, they mainly indicate on which level the micro-dynamics operate. At other places, similarly to the placement of articulation markings, they will be explicitly required when they are unconventional and therefore might not be added by the average performer as a matter of course. This is often the case in the Berlin Sturm und Drang style of the second half of the eighteenth century. In the Mannheim school of Johann Stamitz, long crescendi (more often than diminuendi) appear with increasing frequency. They are not only specified ("crescendo il forte") but can mostly be seen in the instrumentation as well, as more parts are added one after the other. These long crescendi often occur on patterns that are repeated on a higher pitch or on a sustained harmony. J. F. Reichardt describes their effect in his *Briefe eines aufmerksamen Reisenden* (1774, second volume 1776),

> Man erzählet, daß, da Jomelli dieses in Rom zum erstenmale hören ließ, die Zuhörer sich bey dem *crescendo* allmählich von den Sitzen erhoben, und bey dem *diminuendo* erst wieder Luft schöpften, und merkten, daß ihnen der Athem ausgeblieben war. Ich habe diese letztere Wirkung in Manheim an mir selbst empfunden. (It is said that, when Jomelli displayed this effect for the first time in Rome, the listeners gradually lifted themselves up from their chairs during the *crescendo,* and only took breath again with the *diminuendo,* noticing that they had been breathless. I experienced this effect on myself in Manheim.)

Even if this were only a tale, it still clearly indicates that the longer crescendo-diminuendo was new and was experienced as something extraordinary. Reichardt adds that the two great German opera composers of the mid-eighteenth century, Hasse and Graun, never used this device. Mozart only sparingly writes long crescendi; typically it is found in the accompaniment under the final trill of a solo section in a concerto, announcing the tutti entrance of the orchestra. Even in the late G-minor symphony, KV 550 (1788), he asks for a crescendo only twice in the first movement and twice in the trio of the minuet. Toward the end of the eighteenth century and increasingly in the nineteenth century, macro-dynamic effects overshadow micro-dynamics until the latter almost disappear from memory. Micro-dynamics were rediscovered, together with phrasing and articulation principles, when Early Music performance was seriously studied again in the twentieth century.

8. ORCHESTRATION—
INSTRUMENTATION—ARRANGEMENT

The Birth of the Orchestra by John Spitzer and Neal Zaslaw (2004),
The Scoring of Baroque Concertos by Richard Maunder (2004), and
The Essential Bach Choir by Andrew Parrott (2000) are some of the
most valuable recent studies in this field. Though their conclusions
might not convince everybody, they bring a wealth of information,
which mostly confirmed my own findings and experience.

Composers frequently handled orchestration aspects quite freely;
scores do not indicate the number of players per part, and we must
undertake considerable research in order to know the local customs.
The very words "orchestra" and "choir" may be misleading. We assume we know what they mean: a group of players or singers, where
most parts are performed by a number of persons in unison. If the
group is small, we can speak of "chamber choir" or "chamber orchestra." We call "chamber music" the situation where each part is performed individually. Iconographical and historical research and the
surviving performance material demonstrate that the great majority
of baroque concerti and orchestral suites were performed one-to-
a-part; this could be the case even for symphonies. Tutti and solo
specify the function rather than the number of players. Similarly, in
many of Bach's cantatas, the "choir" often seems to have consisted of
one soprano, contralto, tenor and bass each, who frequently also had
to sing their own recitative and/or aria. The orchestra was propor-
tionally small: a maximum of two or three first and second violins,
one or two violas, two or three string basses, organ, and some wind
instruments.

We know of descriptions of specific and sometimes quite unusual occasions. For example, Corelli conducted an orchestra of more than one hundred players in 1705; Mozart performed a symphony with an orchestra of about eighty-five to ninety players in 1781, while an orchestra of only thirty-two players first performed Beethoven's *Eroica* Symphony. These personnel decisions were dependent on the occasion and on the money available. We should realize that the numbers in such specific situations will have had consequences upon the performance itself. In the first half of last century, Willem Mengelberg used a choir of 400–500 singers for Bach's St. Matthew Passion performances, with the full and large Concertgebouw Orchestra of Amsterdam. Some extremely slow tempi, as documented in his 1939 recording of this work, might be the consequence of these large numbers.

Related to the orchestration is the disposition of the ensemble. Is the cantata performed on the church tribune (back or side gallery) or close to the altar? The accompaniment of organ, one or two string basses and bassoon in Bach's church recitatives might be explained by their being positioned on the tribune next to the organ, relatively far from and above the audience, and behind the singer who would stand close to the railing. The same continuo group close to the altar might easily cover the singer's words. In the opera pit, do the first violins sit in one row, with their backs to the audience, while the second violins face the audience? This set-up, largely documented in iconography and in literature, does not necessarily give a badly balanced sound: the second violins usually play in a lower tessitura than the first, but in this positioning, their instruments are directed more efficiently toward the audience. When a classical or romantic concerto is performed, does the orchestra sit on the same level as the soloist, or is the soloist alone on stage with the orchestra in the pit? In his autobiography, published in 1860–61 shortly after his death, Louis Spohr relates that he chose this latter possibility when he played a concerto in the Milan Teatro della Scala in 1816, because of the large volume of the venue. The latter set-up works very well for Mozart's piano concertos, with their rich orchestration. Even the practice of conducting and/or leading has consequences: Is the ensemble led from the first violin, as in the case of the Beethoven *Eroica* mentioned earlier, or from the harpsichord, or is somebody beating time? My experience is that without a conductor, every orchestral player has a far greater autonomy, individuality, and responsibility. Or are there two directors, as was the case in Italian opera up to Verdi's time: *the* conductor for the soloists, and the first violin leading the orchestra (plus possibly a third conductor for the choir, in the wings)? Assessing the practical consequences of these and similar questions is not an easy task. We have to study the sources, experiment, extrapolate, play and listen, and bear in mind that the composers will by necessity have had an empirical approach in light of the different variables. Let us imagine, for example, Bach conducting his Saint Matthew Passion in the Amsterdam Concertgebouw today. Even if he had accepted secular instead of religious surroundings, and assuming that he would have had a free choice, I am not certain that he would have chosen the same forces and set-up as in his Leipzig Saint Thomas church. Nor do I want to say that he would have used Mengelberg's version, which, incidentally, I find very beautiful and touching, though demonstrably "wrong" (against most historically documented evidence) in many details. However, I would guess that had Bach known the size of the hall, the number of performers, and the modern instruments and voices with their specific technique and aesthetics, he might have written something entirely different.

In a number of cases, we do not know the exact significance of the terminology used. Fortunately, research continues to be carried out in this field and shows that meanings can vary in time and place. Conclusions are sometimes unfamiliar or uncomfortable and thus not easily believed, accepted, or integrated into practice. Indeed there really is no agreement yet on a number of issues, although they make substantial difference in sound. Obviously a violone is a big viola— but how big? Is it used as an eight- or sixteen-foot instrument, and with how many strings and in which tuning? Violoncello is a small violone, but how small and with how many strings? Was it always played vertically between the legs, just as the viola da gamba, or could violoncello (with or without the qualifier *piccolo*) actually mean *viola da spalla*? We know that the viola da spalla was played horizontally, hung around the player's neck, but how big could it be, what did it sound like, how many strings did it have, and how was it tuned? For how long and where was it used? From what time does the word violoncello rather refer to our size of violoncello? If it can be shown that up to ca. 1730 violoncello generally meant *viola da spalla,* most "normal" cellos that bear earlier dates would be falsifications or were cut down from bigger instruments (eight-foot violones or *basses de violou*) at a later date. Is *viola all'inglese* the same as our viola? Did the *oboe da caccia* always have the rounded form and brass bell, or could it be straight as the *taille*? *Flauto* usually means recorder until that instrument went out of fashion in the 1730s and 1740s, but why do many of Vivaldi's *flauto* parts look so much like *flauto traverso* parts, though he uses the designation *flauto traverso* elsewhere? Was Vivaldi's *flautino* a little recorder or a flageolet, and in which tonality did it stand? What were Bach's *fiauti d'echo* or Telemann's *flauto pastorale*? Is the voice flute an instrument in d^1 at low pitch, or a normal tenor recorder in c^1 at high pitch—and does it make any difference, or does it matter? Did the *flauto piccolo* play at the four-foot or the two-foot pitch in Mozart's *Entführung*? And again, which type of instrument was it: transverse, recorder-like, or a flageolet?

There is obviously more work to do, and we might never have definitive answers to these questions, but I do not want to assume— all too easily—that our familiar instruments were just as familiar to composers in earlier times. I suppose that composers often used instruments that happened to be at hand and, if necessary, would have adapted their parts. This is indicated by Mozart's comment at the end of the manuscript of the *6 Deutsche Tänze* KV 509 (1787) which he sent to Prague:

> Da ich nicht weis was für Gattung flauto piccolo hier ist, so hab ich es in den Natürlichen ton gesetzt; man kann es allzeit übersetzen.
> (Since I do not know which kind of flauto piccolo you have, I wrote it in the natural key; one can always transpose it.)

In other cases, the technical demands of certain pieces can show which instrument was originally intended, as with Bach's "cello" suites, which, in all likelihood, were written for the (diatonically fin-

gered) viola da spalla instead of the (chromatically fingered) violoncello. This explains some of the peculiarities of these pieces regarding
chords and position changes, which are entirely atypical for the "normal" violoncello technique of that time (and difficult enough for the
modern technique). Some cellists might feel as if "their" great Bach
suites are stolen from them, and some do react rather negatively indeed, but the fact that these suites were written for the viola da spalla
does not mean that it is forbidden to play them on the violoncello; it
just means that this instrument is simply not the first choice, not the
instrument that Bach would have had in mind while composing these
fascinating works. Playing them on the cello is a re-instrumentation
that does not need to be less beautiful or touching.

In chamber or solo music, the instrumentation was not always
exactly specified. Some eighteenth-century French prints state that
the same suite or sonata can be played on flute, violin, oboe, recorder,
musette, or vielle. Certain composers obviously wrote their works
exactly with this multiple-choice aspect in mind, staying within all
these instruments' fields of possibilities. Telemann does not go quite
that far because he seldom specifies more than one alternative. As
with his French colleagues, he confronted the problem that a change
of instrument might also entail a change of tonality; pieces specified
for flute were normally played a minor third higher on the recorder
and vice versa, corresponding to their respective fundamentals d^1 and
f^1. When no or few alternatives were given, it can be illuminating to
see which instruments are *not* mentioned. In other cases the technical features of the music itself can show which instrument was first
intended, even if alternatives are specified by the composer or editor.
Was this habit of mentioning multiple instruments on the title page
only a pragmatic commercial stance? Did composers or their publish-
ers just want their books to be sold? Did they not care so much about
how the music sounded?

To some extent, choosing the instrument and, if necessary, adapting the music to this choice was obviously part of the performer's freedom. Perhaps it did not matter much upon which instrument a composition was performed, provided that the performer knew how to
play the work and possessed "good taste." Another consideration can

be the target market of the print or manuscript; was the work written for the professional or for the amateur musician? Since recordings did not yet exist, amateurs had to be resourceful, and could be perfectly happy playing transcriptions of famous works or of works by famous composers on whatever instrument and without regard to the intrinsic qualities of transcription and performance.

The degree of transcription could vary enormously. Sometimes, a re-instrumentation is no more than that. For example, play a sonata for flute and basso continuo on the oboe instead of on the flute. Even this simple procedure will increase the volume of sound, and thus require another kind of continuo playing or can necessitate an adaptation of the tempo. In other cases, some notes must be changed because of tessitura limitations, or, more drastically, the piece needs to be transposed. Evidently, typical idiomatic passages will sound more convincing on the "original" instrument than on any other; they might even be unplayable on the new instrument. Re-instrumentation might then necessitate structural changes as well, and thus the transcription becomes an arrangement or re-composition.

With composers such as Telemann, Handel, and Bach, we often find different versions of the same work; "recycling" was an accepted compositional technique. Composers might elaborate a previous version, adapt it to a new instrument or ensemble, or underlie a new text, and thus the piece may need some rhythmic and melodic changes. The last version is not by definition the best or definitive version; if the composer had revisited the same piece once more, for whatever occasion or reason, he very likely would have changed it yet again. In some instances a later version might not have survived.

The following excursion about the autograph manuscript of J. S. Bach's A-major sonata for obbligato harpsichord and flute, BWV 1032, illustrates what might happen when a composer revises his works. Bach wrote the entire first movement and the beginning of the second movement on three staves that had remained empty at the bottom of the manuscript pages on which he had already written the concerto for two harpsichords and orchestra, BWV 1062. After the end of the concerto, he used complete pages for the flute sonata's second movement (from measure 6) and final Allegro. From six leaves of manuscript, the strip containing the first movement of the flute sonata (BWV 1032) has been cut off, and thus around forty-six measures, roughly two-fifths of the total length, are missing in the second half of this movement. The strip containing measures 56–62 and also the strip containing, on the recto side, the last two measures of the first movement and, on the verso, measures 1–5 of the second movement had originally also been cut off, but were pasted on again. "NB" signs before and after the gap prove that a replacement sheet must have existed, but this is now lost. The excision must have occurred during J. S. Bach's lifetime, because some notes that had inadvertently been cut away were supplemented by letters in his handwriting. Numerous hypotheses have been suggested, but we will probably never know why this mutilation happened. Was Bach unhappy with it? If so, he could have crossed it out as he did elsewhere in the manuscript. Did this portion of BWV 1032 need to be copied into a fair manuscript at the same time as other people were copying BWV 1062? This method of doing so is quite drastic! Or, perhaps most likely, were there so many corrections that it had become too difficult to read and thus needed to be copied as a replacement?

If we want to play this movement, we have to make a reconstruction. I published and recorded one, and would strongly recommend all students to make their own; it is an excellent exercise. When focusing too much on the reconstruction we might easily fail to notice that the existing portion of the movement seems strangely out of shape. If it did not bear the autograph "di J. S. Bach," it might not be considered authentic. The basic material is quite repetitive, the form is not very strong, there are few modulations, the bass is not very well integrated into the structure, there is not much imitation or counterpoint, and although it is written for three parts (flute, right hand and left hand of the harpsichord), many passages show two-part rather than three-part writing. In some places, however, the music sounds unmistakably like a work by J. S. Bach; typically those passages involve more of the bass line and demonstrate development and imitation between the voices. It looks as if this was still a work in progress, possibly a rewriting of an earlier piece in another form, serving another function and with another instrumentation in mind. Quite possibly this movement had not yet reached a definitive state. The last two movements of the autograph confirm this; they survive completely, but show traces of rather important last-minute corrections and revisions. Unfortunately, no other copies of the work are extant, neither earlier nor later, except for a somewhat awkward transcription of the second movement for violin, violoncello, and basso continuo.

We are accustomed to hearing many re-instrumentations. Indeed, we can consider as such the use of modern instruments and their related techniques instead of their historical counterparts; for example, the use of the modern flute instead of the recorder or the use of the piano instead of the harpsichord. Using the modern flute in place of the traverso can have a stronger transformative effect than changing from traverso to baroque violin. Evidently, playing the modern version of the original instrument was never understood or intended as an arrangement, but as an obvious improvement of the new over the older type of instrument. In his monumental study *Johann Sebastian Bach* (1873–1880), Philipp Spitta writes about

> [D]as Idealinstrument, das Bach für seine Inventionen und Sinfonien, Suiten und Clavierfugen vorschwebte … erst ein Instrument, das die Klangfülle der Orgel mit der Ausdrucksfähigkeit des Clavichords in richtigen Verhältnissen vereinigte, war im Stande, dem Erscheinung zu geben, was in des Meisters Phantasie erklang, wenn er für Clavier componierte. Daß unser moderner Flügel dieses Instrument ist, sieht ein jeder. ([T]he ideal instrument which floated in the mind of Bach for the performance of his Inventions and Sinfonias, suites and keyboard fugues … only an instrument that combined in right proportions the volume of tone of the organ with the expressive quality of the clavichord could be capable of reproducing the image that sounded in the master's imagination, when he composed for the keyboard. Everybody sees that our modern grand piano is exactly that kind of instrument.)

I can understand his opinion, and find it even remarkable that he mentions the clavichord at all. However, would the latest Steinway model not be even better than the 1873 piano, or did Bach secretly dream of a synthesizer or a computer?

It is also interesting to see how later composers used earlier material. Without much hesitation, Bach elaborated on Palestrina or

Vivaldi, Handel paraphrased Muffat, Mozart transcribed Bach and Handel, and Mendelssohn arranged Bach's St. Matthew Passion. They all freely updated these works to their own times and means, just as Webern did in his version of Bach's six-part ricercar from the *Musicalisches Ofper.* Webern, however, probably did not see his instrumentation of the ricercar as the way in which he would normally perform Bach's piece; it appears to be more of a conscious re-composition.

Until well into the twentieth century, there was a widespread belief that history and evolution automatically meant progress. This concept included progress in the arts, from one generation to the next. Perhaps the two World Wars and the prospect of mutually assured destruction by nuclear annihilation shattered that illusion. This focus on progress is frequently—and wrongly—associated with Charles Darwin's *On the Origin of Species by Means of Natural Selection* (1859). He never expressly stated the idea of improvement. On the contrary, it was after Herbert Spencer coined the term "survival of the fittest" in 1864 (which clearly included this idea) that Darwin himself responded in the 1872 edition of *On the Origin of Species by Means of Natural Selection.* Darwin wrote, "I have no good evidence of the existence in organic beings of an innate tendency towards progressive development." Quite remarkably, François-Joseph Fétis, in the prefaces to his first and second editions of the *Biographie Universelle des musiciens* (1835–44, second edition with different preface 1860–65), rejected the concept that in the arts, evolution equals improvement. He describes evolution in the arts as transformation, not as progress. On the other hand, he totally accepted the idea of continuous improvement in the evolution of civilization, science (including art history), and industry (including instrument making).

This is also an important issue in the approach to Early Music. I do not see old instruments or old performing styles and techniques as inherently better or worse than modern ones; it all depends for what repertoire and purpose they are to be used. I am convinced that composers can only write for instruments they have in their ears, not for a "futurophone" that has not yet been invented. Of course, the composer may willingly or unwillingly stretch the limits of what is possible or feasible for the instrument, to which performers and instrument makers will react by trying to find solutions. This may in turn make the composer feel comfortable to go further in stretching the boundaries of the possible, and the cycle will continue.

In my own practice, and with all possible caution and modesty, I attempt to discover which sounds the composer might have heard in his mind while composing, and I try to find the instruments or voices that may correspond best to this. Some problems have no solution; there are no castrato singers anymore, and boys' voices break three or four years earlier than in Bach's time. If I have to choose an alternative to either of these lost voice types, as in the case of a Bach cantata, I often prefer a good, "full" female voice over the "half" falsetto voice of a countertenor, or over an insufficiently trained, all-too-young boy, fully knowing that women, in Bach's day, were not allowed to sing in church. Inevitably, in concert life, we need to make some compromises. In a solo recital I can play five different flutes, but in chamber music or orchestral situations this could become too complicated because each flute might be at a different pitch. All performers must choose how far they want to go.

Even if we do not possess all the construction details of certain instruments, we often know what they did *not* look like, or we have descriptions of their properties and use. I would love to see more of a trial-and-error approach with attempts at informed reconstruction, rather than arbitrary but convenient choices or easy effects. The latter include: percussion instruments added to ensembles, when there is no trace of them to be found in the score, and no suggestion from what we know that they were added ad libitum. Today, when they are added, they are typically given greater prominence and performed with greater invention than is suggested by adherence to existing examples or descriptions. Renaissance music is played on eighteenth-century gambas, and early-seventeenth-century cornetto or violin sonatas are played on completely unhistorical recorders. Often one uses late, more comfortable and familiar types of instruments or techniques for pieces of an earlier generation. Not all these "translations" seem very appropriate or unavoidable—"traduttore traditore" (translator, traitor); so many different types of instruments are being copied that quite often there is the possibility of finding the "right one."

I find this attitude quite disingenuous. Uninformed of such details, audiences are led to believe that this is "how it was" by performers who are not ignorant, but instead choose to ignore such details. The effect is reinforced if the performers have great reputations and if the concerts take place in specialized Early Music festivals. I do know that my position regarding re-instrumentation and arrangements can seem rather purist, but purism is not at all its motivation. In concert or recording performances, I do not want to sell second-rate quality. If I perform an arrangement in whatever form, made by myself or someone else, and notice that the original version is substantially stronger than the arrangement, I feel ashamed toward my audience. Even if the audience does not know the original, I will decide not to play the arrangement anymore. This applies to historical arrangements as well: it is not because some of Mozart's sonatas for violin and piano were published ca. 1800 in a flute version that I automatically consider this arrangement as good. Indeed, the violin version is much more efficient, expressive, rich, and consequent. In my eyes (or in my ears, rather), playing these works on the flute means robbing them of some essential qualities, which I cannot compensate for with "flute-qualities." I need modesty and judgment. Of course, every artist is free to do what he wants. I am not going to decide for him or her what is permitted or forbidden, but neither do I want to give false illusions to the audience (explicitly or implicitly). For me this is a matter of intellectual and artistic honesty.

In the preceding pages, I commented on the conventions pertaining to reading the notation. In the chosen period, these conventions would not have been valid in the same way at all places and times, but at any given time and place a well-trained musician could be expected to understand what to do. It was mainly a question of knowing the key(s) to read the notation.

A next question is, how was a musician expected to supplement the notation, according to his own will, insight, and abilities? Though often not explicitly written into the score, basso continuo realization, ornaments, and cadenzas belong to the way a performer needs to read and understand the notation.

9. BASSO CONTINUO

The manner in which the basso continuo—one of the determining elements of baroque music—is realized is continuously under debate, in theory as well as in practice. The figures only indicate which harmony is desired, but many questions remain unanswered. Which (combinations of) instruments are to be used? Must there always be a string bass, and if so, which one? In France, a viola da gamba seems to have been included in the standard continuo group of a chamber ensemble until that instrument went out of fashion. In other countries, title pages of sonata prints often mention "violone *o* cembalo"—not "*e*"; frequently the bass part is marked "cembalo" only. Should we take these indications literally, or assume that these composers did not mean what they wrote? C. P. E. Bach, in the second part of his *Versuch* (1762), states that harpsichord plus violoncello form the ideal continuo group, but is this valid for the entire basso continuo era, 1600–1800? Anyway, he also mentions in his autobiography that he accompanied Frederick the Great "all alone" at the keyboard on (at least) one occasion. Which position or tessitura, which rhythm, which number of voices should we choose in our realization? Can the harmony be further enriched by dissonances? I am not sure that the frequent *acciaccature,* documented in French and in Italian continuo realizations should be used in all genres, from chamber music to opera or church music. Should we adopt a more chordal or more melodically oriented and ornamental style? Should the chords be played together or arpeggiated, and if arpeggiated, in which way and how fast? In his *Versuch* (1752), Quantz prescribes arpeggi only as a means of accentuating the strongest dissonances, but now I hear them everywhere,

Figure 3. J. S. Bach, *Largo e dolce* from Sonata for Obbligato Harpsichord and Transverse Flute, BWV 1030 (ca. 1736–37), mm. 9–16. With kind permission of the Staatsbibliothek zu Berlin, Musikabteilung mit Mendelssohn-Archiv (D-BS, Mus.ms. Bach P 975).

and in fact they were often used with the opposite aim of softening the consonances. Should the top part of the realization always stay below the solo part's notes? What about unisons with or imitations of the solo part?

We are fortunate that J. S. Bach or his students wrote out quite a number of continuo passages. They are usually very full. Even in chamber music we see four-part more often than three-part harmony, occasionally even enriched with one or more extra notes on important points. Voice-leading is strict, logical, and efficient; that this had his attention is made clear by the fact that in his autographs each voice has its own beams; he usually writes no vertical chords (see figure 3). If the harmony is obvious, the right hand may pause on the strong beats. Quite often the realization lies high, frequently passing over the solo part. More complicated or melodic figurations occur mainly during the solo part's long notes or silences. I suppose that Bach wrote out some continuo passages instead of writing figures over the left hand, when he wanted the realization to be integrated into the rest of the composition. This is clearly the case in some of his sonatas for obbligato harpsichord and flute, violin, or viola da gamba. I regret that this style of continuo playing is not heard more frequently in today's Bach performances. In fact, it seems also applicable to many of his contemporaries since it basically reflects what is taught in many historical basso continuo treatises.

Unfortunately, and in my opinion wrongly, some performers see these treatises as no more than a theoretical guide toward correct harmonization, without practical artistic value; others discern local schools and an evolution in time. We can expect that also in earlier times, basso continuo realization, being improvised, was very personal. The danger of this assumption is that we follow only our own taste, or the taste of some famous keyboard or plucked instruments players, thus establishing a kind of fashionable "secondhand" style, which by itself can work very well, but does not need to be historically relevant. The frequent inclusion of a large group of continuo players (with keyboards, plucked, string and wind instruments, together or in alternation) in rather small ensembles seems to be one such instance. This certainly lends colors to the performance, but not infrequently the packaging becomes more brilliant than the contents. The attention is then drawn to the continuo rather than to the solo playing. In my opinion this totally inverts the hierarchy. Just as historical treatises inform us about the desired treatment of the voice or the instruments, careful reading of the continuo treatises and putting their advice into practice at appropriate places logically should form the basis of basso continuo teaching and playing.

10. ORNAMENTATION

Neal Zaslaw presents an interesting case study: "Ornaments for Corelli's violin sonatas, op. 5" in *Early Music* (February 1996).

Quantz's distinction, clearly expressed in his *Versuch* (1752), between "wesentliche Manieren" and "willkürliche Veränderungen" is a convenient starting point. The latter can be translated as "arbitrary alternatives," that is, substitutions of one note or passage by another, freely invented by the performer. Quantz reserves their use for the soloist who knows the rules of composition. The former, the "essential ornaments," on the other hand, are judged as being indispensable to all good performance. This category includes all ornaments that can be indicated by special signs or small printed notes: appoggiaturas, trills, mordents, and so forth. We see that in the later seventeenth and eighteenth centuries, many composers developed their own set of signs for them. In France, more or less up to the French Revolution, these ornaments were mostly written into the score in great detail, in Germany much less often (except for lute and keyboard music), and in England and Italy even less often. This does not necessarily mean that in England or Italy these ornaments were less frequently used—they were simply more frequently left to the performer's discretion. Though the rules obviously differ considerably with person, instrument, time, and place, the correct interpretation (form, length, timing on or before the beat, dynamics) and character of these ornaments are explained in countless treatises, charts, and prefaces. With some study and practice, a sensitive musician should be able to integrate them into any non-ornamented piece, according to the style of the composer and to the instrument. It is often forgotten that Quantz calls them "essential": even if they are not expressly written, we cannot do without them! As always, the ultimate rule is "good taste."

Let me continue the comparison of music and language. Since "essential" ornaments usually occur on one single note, they operate on the level of the syllable, of the articulation. These ornaments most often express the initial consonant(s) or vowel of a syllable; sometimes (as in a trill with resolution) they link one syllable to the next. Thus, when performed well, they should create diversity and make us understand the text, both acoustically and emotionally. In this sense "essential" is correct; it is essential that an ornament is performed, though the choice of a particular kind of ornament is sometimes less essential.

In my experience, the music of Lully and his followers, active all over Europe, has suffered severely from a lack of understanding of this principle. The score, with only the occasional trill, looks dry, simple, neutral, bare, for singers as well as for instrumentalists. I suppose we really have to clothe this music. Fortunately concurrent singing and instrumental schools give us a wealth of information about what ornaments were typically added in particular situations. These ornaments are essential for a "just" image of Lully's style: without them, his music is mostly judged unattractive, by listeners as well as by scholars who only read the score. Interestingly, the original orchestral parts used by Lully and other opera composers give us little more information. The musicians will have remembered what to play, rather than having to write it down, as even today's specialist orchestra members might prefer to do. These ornaments belonged to the unwritten part of music, the part associated with common knowledge, daily practice, mother tongue, and good taste.

I want to single out one ornament that was mentioned earlier: vibrato. In our modern tradition, vibrato is omnipresent, belongs to every note, and is essential to emotional expression—pity the poor pianists who must do without! In the seventeenth through the nineteenth centuries, for singers and for instrumentalists, vibrato was considered an ornament to be used on one single long note, and not to be misused or overused. Its general adoption in singing and playing dates from the end of the nineteenth and the beginning of twentieth century (Fritz Kreisler is frequently credited for it in violin playing), and many instruments (clarinet, brass) only started to use it much later. Together with its increasing use, the size of the oscillation increased and the speed decreased, even at the risk of masking the intended pitch. As with all ornaments, its use in earlier times will have depended on time, place, personal temperament, instrument, context, function, size of concert venue, and so on.

Nowadays, Geminiani is often quoted as requesting vibrato on every note, and as such his writing is used to infer the general fashion of his time. This oversimplification probably originated with violinists, who, being used to continuous vibrato, happily took up the master's advice. In his *Rules for Playing in a True Taste* (ca. 1748), Geminiani tells the flautist to vibrate only on long notes (unfortunately, we are not told by which means: finger or breath). On the violin, though, the vibrato "*may* be made on any Note whatsoever" (my italics). In *The Art of Playing on the Violin* (1751), he shows how various kinds of vibrato should be used for different affects or for making short notes "more agreable". It is somewhat unclear whether his concluding remark "for this Reason it should be made use of as often as possible" is a general advice or refers to short notes only. Interestingly, Geminiani appears to be quite alone with this statement; he might have been as eccentric in his use of vibrato as in his rubato playing. When Robert Bremner, one of Geminiani's former students, republished his master's violin treatise (1777, reissued by Preston & Son after 1789), he left out exactly this passage on vibrato. In the 1777 preface to Schetky's quartets op. 6, Bremner also condemns the use of vibrato except as an occasional ornament. As we have seen, Tartini, in his *Traité des Agréments* (before 1756), even requires the long notes performed with *messa di voce* to be played absolutely without vibrato, in order not to disturb the purity of tuning. Throughout the eighteenth and nineteenth century and all over Europe, vibrato seems to have moved in and out of fashion. Some performers or schools were attacked for applying vibrato too frequently; generally, good taste required that it should only be used in solo singing or playing and even then very moderately applied on long notes only.

Whereas at least one modern conductor (Sir Roger Norrington) has his orchestra play without vibrato for nineteenth-century repertoire—an interesting case of crossover—few of today's Early Music singers or players go very far in that direction. Many are happy to just reduce its frequency of use and its size. I very much regret this lack of courage and this lack of curiosity toward sound ideals that speak so clearly from the old treatises. Of course, "forgetting" to vibrate supposes that we focus on something else, on the violinist's right hand instead of the left; on the flautist's or singer's breath; on the invention of sound and its continuous creation, shape, and expression throughout a longer note. As mentioned earlier, vibrato was usually not included on notes performed with the *messa di voce*; however, it could be present as an ornament in the actual performance of a long note, provided that this note lies in a solo part and has enough expressive potential.

Quantz's second category, "willkürliche Veränderungen" translated as "arbitrary alternatives," operates more on the level of singing than of speaking. When one note is not enough to express the full emotional undercurrent of the text, adding a florid ornament will help us. The "willkürliche Veränderungen" should thus be suspended from strong syllables and meaningful words, and be the inner consequence thereof. All these ornamental notes cannot sound equally full, because then they would all become essential, and all would merit their own syllable—hence the diminuendo within a vocalize or slur we have already spoken about. Even if these ornaments were prepared and notated, with or without precision, they should sound as if the performer spontaneously invented them, and they should possess the emotional motivation of the moment. Otherwise the groups of notes become scale or arpeggio exercises. Ideally, we should not ornament a passage twice in the same way. How different these individual ornamentations can look is exemplified by the many extant ornamented versions of slow movements from Corelli's violin sonatas op. 5 (1700). To begin with, the Amsterdam print of 1710 gives Corelli's own way of playing—at least this is what the publisher purports, inviting non-believers to come and see Corelli's autograph manuscript in his possession. Even so, we should bear in mind that Corelli would not always have played the same ornaments. Various printed and manuscript sources until the end of the eighteenth century include completely different ornaments for some of these movements. While these later versions might not be too useful at teaching us about Corelli's own practice, they are certainly a good overview of the stylistic evolution of ornaments throughout the eighteenth century.

There are many methods for learning to invent "Willkürliche Veränderungen": we can look at some "recipe books" where each interval is shown with a series of possible ornamentations or diminutions, and we can study examples of a simple melody with its ornamented version underneath, such as Telemann's *Sonate Metodiche* (1728 and 1732) (see figure 4). We certainly must realize that many elaborate passages in compositions are in fact only written-down ornamentations, and should therefore be performed as such. When these passages are no more than "arbitrary alternatives," we may feel free to replace them by our own inventions. Indeed, there exist many sources of favorite opera arias where the composer's ornamentation has been changed or supplemented by a famous eighteenth-, nineteenth-, and even early-twentieth-century singer, who was unhindered by any exaggerated respect for Urtext versions. We can still hear some of this practice in the earliest opera aria recordings with sopranos such as Adelina Patti and Luisa Tetrazzini. I suppose that this freedom of changing or adding ornamentation was considered the soloist's prerogative, at least in the Italian tradition up to the beginning of the twentieth century.

Gluck's endeavor to have the singers perform what he had written and no more, as expressed in the preface to the 1769 edition of *Alceste*, must often have remained wishful thinking. This important preface quite eloquently describes the then current style of vocal composition and performance: the composer had to allow the singer ample opportunity to show off his or her virtuoso abilities with elaborate *passaggi* and free ornamentation. Gluck accuses composers of complicity because they all too willingly cater to the singer's vanity. Gluck's reforms are aimed precisely at stopping this abuse, as he calls it. One year later, in the preface to *Elena e Paride* (Vienna, 1770) Gluck enumerates the "bad" practices once more: holding a note longer or shorter than written (arbitrary rubato), failing to observe an accelerando or crescendo (these would normally have been the singer's decision, not the composer's), and ill-chosen appoggiaturas, trills, and coloraturas (again

Figure 4. G. Ph. Telemann, *Adagio* from *Sonata Metodica* II for Violin or Transverse Flute and Basso Continuo, TWV 41:A3 (1728), mm. 1–11.

introduced by the performer, not the composer). Gluck states that whereas these effects would do no harm to other composers' works or even improve them, they ruin his own compositions—not exactly a modest stance!

A practical example of what singers would add to the printed text can be found in Domenico Corri's *A Select Collection of the Most Admired Songs, Duets etc. from Operas in the Highest Esteem* (vol. I–III ca. 1780, vol. IV after 1794, vol. V as part II of his singing treatise 1810). Corri was a student of the famous Nicola Porpora, and was himself an influential singing teacher in England. In this collection he prints many favorite recitatives and arias, together with the way a number of great singers performed them. One of his examples is Gluck's famous *Che farò senza Euridice* from *Orfeo ed Euridice* (1762), as sung by Gaetano Guadagni, who was Gluck's first Orfeo—with the singer's ornaments (and the rhythmic adaptation we mentioned earlier)! In the introduction to the first volume, Corri laments the insufficient notation of all the expressive devices (ornaments, rhythm, even pitches), and tries to remedy this by introducing new symbols. He writes,

> Experience has evinced that, for want of such signs, the music of half a century back is in great measure lost to the present time, even in the same country, and is at all times totally unintelligible to a foreign nation.

There seems to be little hope for us, two centuries later!

Some pieces are clearly written as an open and urgent invitation to the performer; without ornamentation they sound too simple and inexpressive. Where do we expect these free ornaments? In vocal music they occur mostly on words with strong emotional meaning—and on good vowels. In French baroque opera they are typically found on *gloire, victoire*, etc. We see them used more in slow rather than in fast instrumental movements. If used in fast movements, they often take the form of an even more virtuosic passage, whereas in slow movements the note values might be less regular or less defined. The Brussels Royal Conservatory library houses a number of violin concertos by Franz Benda (1709–1786), with his own "variationes," as he calls them, for both fast and for slow movements. They are excellent examples of the extent to which ornamentation could be applied. Other typical situations are the da capo of an opera aria (where ornamentation was a "must") and the repeat of an idea or section. In his *Versuch* (1752), Quantz advises to perform the idea simply at first, then ornamented the subsequent times, so that the audience can hear that the ornamentation is the invention of the interpreter, not of the composer. Quantz states also that in trio sonatas or duets, the ornamentation in one upper part must generally be imitated, not negated or exaggerated by the second melodic voice. This is illustrated in Telemann's *Trietti Metodichi* (1731).

Doubles present a special case. They originate with the seventeenth-century French air de cour, where the second of the two text couplets was even more highly ornamented, in an often rhythmically very intricate way. We find the same style in some French instrumental pieces of the period. J. S. Bach occasionally wrote *doubles* in his instrumental works, sometimes more with "wesentliche Manieren," in other places with very virtuoso "willkürliche Veränderungen." These *doubles* always come after the simple version, as a quasi-independent piece. C. P. E. Bach writes an number of keyboard *Sonaten mit veränderten Reprisen* (1760), where the repeat sections are written out in a very freely ornamented way. It can be hard to recognize where the repeat actually starts, since even the left hand is often changed, though the basic harmony evidently remains the same.

Treatises usually stress that in order to invent good "willkürliche Veränderungen," one has to know the rules of composition: free ornamentation must not only be interesting and expressive but also harmonically correct and well integrated in the complete piece. As with the "wesentliche Manieren," as a final requisite, "good taste" is often quoted. Burney gives a very interesting definition of the concept of taste when he explains musical terminology in an appendix to his *Music, Men and Manners in France and Italy* (1770),

> Taste is the adding, diminishing, or changing a melody, or passage, with judgment and propriety, and in such a manner as to *improve* it; if this were rendered an invariable rule in what is commonly called *gracing*, the passages, in compositions of the first class, would seldom be changed.

("Diminishing" is used here as in the sixteenth and seventeenth centuries: diminutions occur when longer notes are broken into shorter note values in performance.) Though good taste must go further than faithfully sticking to the written notes, C. P. E. Bach also mentions in his *Versuch* (1753) that the free ornamentation of which a performer is so proud might well have been an idea that the composer had also considered but rejected!

Obviously there is a mutual relationship between the degree of ornamentation and the tempo of a movement. In the Berlin *Empfindsamer Stil* of the second half of the eighteenth century, the inclusion of more and more free ornaments in the *Adagio* must have resulted in the tempo slowing down. Conversely, the predilection for very slow *Adagios* gave the performer room for extensive ornamentation, as in the above-mentioned Benda violin concertos. The slow movements of *empfindsam* concertos are especially unconvincing in an unornamented form, and the practice of adding extensive ornamentation continued well into the classical era. An interesting ornamented version of the slow movement of Mozart's A-major piano concerto KV 488 (1786) survives; though not in his hand, it seems to come from Mozart's estate, suggesting that Mozart knew of it—he might have prepared it for a student.

The question of which free ornaments to add is often the first to be asked by a "modern" performer desiring to treat an early composition "correctly." In my opinion, it should be the last question to be asked. First, all other aspects must be understood. Otherwise, ornaments are no more than a shiny but thin veneer applied to a fundamentally "modern" concept.

11. CADENZAS

Related to freely improvised ornamentation are the cadenzas and fermatas, which occur in arias, sonatas, and concerti. Whereas fermatas are performed on one single chord, usually a dominant seventh, and are thus limited to one basic harmony, a cadenza occurs on the succession of a $^6_4$ and a $^5_3$ chord on the dominant, just before the end of a piece or a solo. Both should be invented on the spot, or at least sound as if they were improvised, even if the performer prepared them and wrote them down. Cadenzas became fashionable with singers, first in Italy around 1715, later in Germany and England, too, and were quickly adopted by instrumentalists, who were imitating singers as they were supposed to do.

According to Quantz's *Versuch* (1752), cadenzas should be short, fresh, performed without regular tempo or meter, and surprising, as a last "bon mot" in a speech. Generally, cadenzas for singers and wind instrumentalists should be performed in one breath, those for strings can be somewhat longer, and those for keyboard, offering most possibilities for modulation and imitation, can be longest. Cadenzas for more than one soloist are usually longer, too, and are naturally seldom improvised. In his *Traité des Agrémens* (probably written before 1756), Tartini expressed the view that the cadenza is not the most interesting part of a piece, but since the audience wants it, the performer must be able to invent it. Tartini's cadenza examples are, not unexpectedly, rather discrete: a good flautist could often still perform them in one breath. Historical examples confirm this image. They also show that vocal, wind, and string cadenzas are seldom thematically linked to the piece itself. If they are, they are usually not the most success-

ful; the short duration allows little more than a literal quotation of a
motive, plus some leading in and out and the final trill. Besides the
usual short ones, we do find some extraordinary long violin cadenzas,
rather caprice than cadenza, by Vivaldi and Tartini himself. The fast
movements of Locatelli's violin concertos op. 3 (ca. 1733) comprise
an elaborate and often extremely difficult *Capriccio*, which curiously
ends with the word *Cadenza*; after a long, breakneck display of virtuosity, the performer is supposed to improvise his or her own cadenza,
probably shorter and maybe more melodical than the *Capriccio* itself.
Bach's harpsichord cadenza for the fifth Brandenburg concerto is an
example of an unusually long cadenza, even among keyboard cadenzas, and resembles these caprice-cadenzas. A collection of original
keyboard cadenzas by C. P. E. Bach shows that while the longer cadenzas can be linked to the piece itself, they do not need to be so. The
shorter cadenzas are, at most, based upon a little motive, which is
even then usually not literally quoted. Some of C. P. E. Bach's shorter
cadenzas are restricted to the right hand alone. Mozart's keyboard
cadenzas are often thematic, highly inventive, and rather long. According to his wife, they were written for his students. He himself
would presumably have improvised one—and each time another one.
When composer-performers write cadenzas, they obviously want to
introduce more facets of their themes and have invention enough to
combine and stage them. In that sense, it is a pity that we do not have
Mozart's cadenzas for his violin, oboe or flute concerti. Would they
also have been longer than the average two lines? We find only one
cadenza for a single melody instrument written out by Mozart, in the
slow movement of *Ein musikalischer Spass* KV 522 (1787). It is not ex-
cessively long, but was certainly meant as a caricature: we could learn
what to avoid. A short vocal cadenza stands at the end of Mozart's
Solfeggio KV 393/5 (1782?). Though it has not been recognized as such
by the composer of the bass part (that was absent in Mozart's manuscript), it clearly is a splendid example of an almost instrumental $^6_4$—$^5_3$
cadenza. It could easily be taken as a model for melodic instrument
cadenzas. Caprice-cadenzas for winds are extremely rare. Charles
Delusse published twelve of them in his *L'Art de la Flute traversière*
(1761). This whole flute method is strongly dependent on the Gemin-

iani violin method of 1751, which had appeared in a French translation in Paris in 1752. Possibly Delusse imitated the Italian violin idiom also in his *Caprices.* Even an acclaimed virtuoso flautist such as F. Devienne (1759–1803) kept his cadenzas within the one-breath length, as far as we can judge from his written-out examples.

It is interesting to see how fast style can change. Beethoven's cadenza for Mozart's D-minor piano concerto KV 466 is as typical for Beethoven as it is atypical for Mozart. Later in the nineteenth and twentieth centuries we see many of these collage-cadenzas, where the styles of cadenza and concerto do not match anymore, and where string or wind cadenzas are as long and ambitious as piano cadenzas. Also today, even Early Music wind and string performers are very much tempted by this romantic image of the instrumental hero—we only rarely hear cadenzas in eighteenth-century repertoire whose style corresponds to documented eighteenth-century practice. Might these performers be afraid to disappoint the listeners, who are of course also more accustomed to the elaborate romantic virtuoso cadenzas?

Just as for the "willkürliche Veränderungen," there are two facets to cadenza playing: they can be correctly composed, but it is the actual playing which will make them good or bad. We must thus "decode" the notated cadenzas. According to Quantz, their true performance cannot be notated.

Though improvisation is per definition not notated, it often could start from a written-down theme (as in a thematic cadenza or in improvised variations) or it could afterward be notated, probably in a somewhat more organized and cleaned-up form (as in the case of Bach's Musicalisches Opfer, BWV 1079). *The fact that many pieces might have originated as improvisations will inevitably influence their performance.*

12. IMPROVISATION

Most great composers were great improvisers, too. Very likely, they will have included a great deal of improvisation in playing their own compositions, or varied their pieces from one performance to another, not only in the field of free ornamentation or cadenzas. It is known that Handel included quite a lot of improvisation in his organ concertos, which could explain the fact that in the posthumous published set of concertos opus 7, some movements or sections are missing.

We can suppose that compositions named *Fantasia, Caprice, Toccata, Prélude non mesuré,* and so forth will resemble improvisational style. Some are notated freely, without barlines, others fully measured. In the absence of sound recordings, descriptions such as C. P. E. Bach's chapter *Von der freyen Fantasie,* in the second part of his *Versuch über die wahre Art, das Clavier zu spielen* (1762), can give us an idea of performance. Some of Froberger's *toccatas* resemble the *prélude non mesuré* very much, but are notated with great precision and can thus serve as a model for the latter. Quite a number of improvisers, among them J. S. Bach and Mozart, were famous not only for their free fantasias, but also for their fugato playing. Who would not want to have been present when Bach visited Frederick the Great in Potsdam and improvised over the king's theme and later over a theme of his own, or when Schubert was improvising during one of the famous Schubertiades, or Chopin in a Parisian salon?

It is not enough to decode the notation appropriately, we must also judge the source's authority and the value of the information it transmits. This is a delicate but necessary exercise that cannot be brought to a good end by science alone.

13. MANUSCRIPT—PRINT— REVISION—MODERN EDITIONS

Music was mostly written for immediate use, not for eternity, and certainly not in view of a scientific edition in our times. Anybody who has handled old manuscripts and prints will have experienced how many mistakes they contain—especially notational details such as unclear and inconsistent positioning of articulation and dynamics marks. Some are very good, such as the manuscript of J. S. Bach's violin soli BWV 1001–1006 (see figure 5) or many French engraved editions of the first half of the eighteenth century, but unfortunately this is the exception, not the rule. Even autographs were often quickly penned, and are faulty and error-strewn. Obviously, details were not always considered of much importance, and anyway, when questions arose, the composer or one of his competent students or contemporaries would likely be present when the performance took place, or performers would be acquainted with the style.

Composers such as Johann Sebastian Bach and, even more so, his son Carl Philipp Emanuel Bach are notorious for constantly revising their works. The latter's own copies of his printed keyboard works partly survive; they are scribbled full of alternatives, ornamentations, and elaborations that clearly do not all date from the same time period. This is a nightmare for any editor. Some of C. P. E. Bach's compositions exist in several manuscript and/or printed sources, with different titles, tempi, tonalities, instrumentation, and/or additional movements. Typical examples are his violoncello concerti, which he recomposed later for harpsichord and for flute; not only has the solo part been drastically changed and adapted to

Figure 5. J. S. Bach, *Adagio* from Sonata for Violin Solo, BWV 1001 (1720). With kind permission of the Staatsbibliothek zu Berlin, Musikabteilung mit Mendelssohn-Archiv (D-BS, Mus.ms. Bach P 967).

the new instrument, but he sometimes even changed the orchestral parts.

J. S. Bach also often reworked earlier pieces, as is shown in many religious cantatas, masses, and passions. Other examples are his transcriptions of the violin concerti for harpsichord, or the violin sonata BWV 1019, which does not contain the same movements in all versions. Bach's viola da gamba sonata BWV 1027 was originally a triosonata for two flutes (or violins?) and basso continuo; three movements of this sonata also exist in an organ version, not proven to be by Bach, but certainly from his circle. The very concept of an original, definitive, or best version did not seem to exist at the time.

Even if a genealogy of the sources can be established, this does not necessarily reflect the composer's priorities. A wealthy court with large orchestra, a special occasion such as princely weddings or funerals, and important church festivals could provide the occasion for more lavish rewritings of existing compositions. Would Vivaldi have disapproved of his violin concerti, originally scored with only string and basso continuo accompaniment, being performed by the famous Dresden court orchestra, with added wind ripieni (under the direction of Pisendel, who was probably responsible for those extra parts)? Or would Vivaldi have been so impractical as to always require this richly orchestrated version, once it had been assembled? The presence of a new singer was often reason enough to discard an aria and compose another one. Since style and fashion were changing rapidly, composers could easily feel the need to update their works or, on occasion, works by other composers.

A well-edited and clearly printed modern edition looks dangerously definitive and trustworthy; it seems to leave no room for doubt. Famous virtuosi prepared many modern editions and freely put their own interpretations into the score, as if the purchaser of the edition was fundamentally ignorant and incapable of thinking for himself. In the case of Urtext editions, an expert editor, usually a musicologist rather than a performing musician, has "solved" the problems, and the performer is expected to believe him. Usually, the critical comments are hard to read, often published separately, and intended more for fellow editors and scholars than for performers. It can be done differently: I requested from the editors that my Urtext editions include a separate chapter with performance suggestions based on historical sources. In the musical text I draw special attention to problematical places and unsolved questions, encouraging performers to make their own decisions.

We should use Urtext editions more as the beginning of our investigations into a piece than as the version that we strictly have to adhere to. If we play them as *the truth and nothing but the truth,* we are certain to miss a great deal. I do think that a responsible performer, especially, but not only of Early Music, should study the scientific editions and their critical comments, but also see the sources for himself. He can then formulate his own conclusions or preferences, discuss them with colleagues and test them in rehearsals and concerts, in order to come to "valid" but necessarily always temporary solutions. Each performance is unique. Even for the very best modern editions, the title of this essay holds true: the notation *is not* the music!

The way the notation is read—and thus the performance itself—also depends on the general cultural environment wherein the performer stands. Consequently, even if those topics seem to be only laterally linked to our study of the notation, the audience's as well as the performer's attitude must be considered. We must examine the difference between emotion and affect and their transmission toward the audience, and finally the two-fold concept of authenticity must be discussed.

14. THE AUDIENCE'S ATTITUDE

Professional musicians were normally employed in the service of a court, town, or church, and thus did not enjoy complete independence. The character, the degree of education (musical and otherwise), and the social class of the audience or employer, and the local etiquette, and expectations inevitably had their effect on both the composer and the performer. In this respect, nothing has changed very much: I do not play similarly before a small gathering of connoisseurs as I would in a large concert hall with a non-specialist audience. I consider recording to be still another matter. There I am confronted by a lonely microphone as my sole link to a future and unknown audience. In a concert I can play in a more extreme, exuberant, or overwhelming way, but if put onto CD, this is very likely to grow stale upon repeated hearing. I somehow prefer to leave some room for the CD listener's creative fantasy and participation.

Some examples in order to illustrate how performers have dealt with this, willingly or unwillingly:

· In the French musical style around the court of Louis XIV, a display of virtuosity was not held in high esteem; it lacked the idiosyncratic balance between noble simplicity and gracefulness, which is encountered in all French art forms of that era. François Couperin expresses this aristocratic attitude very eloquently in the preface to his *Pièces de Clavecin* (1713): "j'ayme beaucoup mieux ce qui me touche que ce qui me surprend" (I prefer very much that what touches me over that what surprises me). I would consider this as the credo of French music until ca. 1725. The Concerts Spirituels, which were held in the Paris Tuileries from 1725 onward, created a completely different context: they were public concerts in a larger venue, for a paying audience. They were thus economically dependent on the audience's taste and appreciation—and this audience was no longer solely the court. Though originally set up in order to present religious music on the days when there was no opera performance, they eventually offered many Italian and other foreign virtuosos a stage where they could shine, delight, and surprise their listeners. Without originally having been set up for this, the Concerts Spirituels were instrumental in changing the French musical taste.

· We know from numerous descriptions that during an opera performance the audience was not always as respectfully silent as most are today. Audiences could be talking, eating, walking in and out (not unlike today's movie theater patrons), and occasionally, when the great star singer had a favorite aria, they would listen and cry for a repeat. The opera was as much or more a social as an artistic event: people went to the theatre to be seen as much as to see. On the other hand, libretti were sold, even in cantata services, so that interested listeners could follow the text.

· The audience was not always on the winning side, though. The existence of specific rules in private music societies such as the Berlin Akademien in the second half of the eighteenth century is telling: arrive on time, no smoking, no eating or drinking, no talking . . . obviously conduct needed to be and could be enforced.

· Similarly, Spohr relates in his *Selbstbiografie* (published in 1860–1861), that at the Stuttgart court, during concerts, the king and his entourage were accustomed to playing cards, without paying much attention to the music, even without remaining silent. When Spohr was invited to perform there in 1807 or 1808, he was famous enough to require and obtain that the playing tables be pushed aside and the audience admonished to keep silent and listen.

· And from more recent times: this is what Lord Reith, the first Director-General of the BBC, gave as a guideline to the young musicologist Denis Stevens joining the famous BBC Third Programme services, ca. 1950, "We know precisely what the public wants, and by Heaven they're not going to get it!"

15. THE PERFORMER'S ATTITUDE

Very often, musicians from earlier centuries performed in situations that would not inspire envy today: during meals, receptions, and balls, in the open air, on the water (Handel)—merely as background noise. I suppose not everybody reacted in the same way to these circumstances; probably some were disengaged and wanted to do nothing more than their duty, while others tried to attract attention nevertheless, by singing or playing in a flashy virtuoso style, loud, and full of many grand gestures. Obviously, the "standard" performer does not and did not exist. His temperament, capabilities and ambition, his education within specific conventions of culture and social class, and his particular function and performance context will have shaped his attitude. If he is "only" a performer, he might be less adventurous (or less successful) in adding his own layer of interpretation to an existing piece than if he is a competent composer, able to expand upon his own works or remodel other people's compositions.

It is interesting to look at the quite complicated relationship between the three poles upon which music rests: composer, performer, and audience. How did composers and audiences expect musicians to act, read, and execute the music? Were they to stay faithful to the notation or to freely expand it through adding their own ornaments and expressive devices? Let us examine the performer's rights, responsibilities, and duties from different angles.

a. The Amateur Versus the Professional

Basically, and allowing for exceptions, today as well as in earlier times, the amateur plays for his own pleasure and has no responsibilities toward anybody: the composer is mostly not present, and if someone else wants to listen, that is entirely the listener's problem. One could say that the amateur plays with a profoundly egotistical attitude, as much a consumer as any CD buyer or concertgoer. Even when he occasionally plays before an audience, he will generally be focused more on his personal satisfaction of playing in public ("like a professional") than on the adequate rendering of the score or the interaction with the listeners.

The professional, on the contrary, plays for other people's pleasure: his audience's. They bought a ticket, dressed up, traveled to the concert venue, and they want to enjoy the event. Clearly this gives the performer another, heavier responsibility. Just like any salesman, he will be identified with the quality of his product. Of course, though the professional performer's private pleasure is not his main goal, if he takes no pleasure in his job, he will soon burn out, eventually become bitter and unhappy, disenchanted and disenchanting, and will sooner or later (hopefully sooner) stop performing altogether.

It is the professional musician who interests us here. He often seems to balance on a tightrope stretched between the audience on one side and the composer on the other. Both sides need him. Composers need performers in order for their music to be heard, and listeners require performers in order to hear what the composer has written. Most audiences cannot read a musical score and hear it immediately and accurately in the mind's ear. Performers are dependent on both composers and audiences. Most do not compose their own music; therefore they need somebody else to write it for them. Performers also need the audience. They want to be on stage and feel the electrifying contact with their listeners. They move the emotions of their listeners, and hope, in return, to be admired by them.

b. The Compass

Let us imagine a horizontal line on a map, and put the audience at the one end, west, and the composer at the other end, east (see figure 6). In respect to this line the performer can choose a number of different positions:

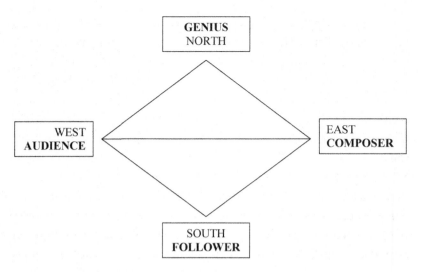

Figure 6. The Performer's Positioning.

- North, above the line, I would place those performers who somehow believe themselves to be superior to the composer and/or the audience.
- South, below the line, I place performers who see themselves as subservient to the composer and/or audience.
- West, I place the performer who pays most attention to the audience.
- East, I place the performer who pays more attention to the composer.

Though some (and maybe the more interesting) musicians frequently change places, others seem to be happy with their once-chosen position. Some typical cases:

- First there is the performer who does not seek to impose himself, who respectfully wants to stay in the shadow of the composer. He would like to make himself anonymous and only be the composer's instrument. He will most often safely limit himself to the printed text, preferably an Urtext edition, with minimum personal interpretation and maximum neutrality (although that is an illusion, of course). We could picture him very east, below the composer's position, below the line.

· Also below the line, but in the extreme west below the audience, I would put the "seducer." He is the performer who above all wants to please and flatter the audience, and who does not ask any effort from the listener (or not more than the three-minute time span familiar to television and radio). His repertoire consists of hits, the best of, and so forth. He will freely adapt anything, without really caring too much what the composer actually wrote, as long as the audience recognizes the tune and reacts favorably toward him.

· A third position is that of the "genius." He considers himself to have full power over the compositions, to be at least as important as the composer, and as such does not feel all too responsible to him. As a true hero of the concert platform he masterfully captivates his audience. He has an immediately recognizable and inimitable style and sound. Of course, if he is genuinely a superb artist with a very rich and generous personality, listening to his performance can be a marvelous experience. He might reveal more to us about himself than about the piece or its composer, but if he really is as much or possibly even more a genius than the composer, why should we complain? I would put him way up north, well above the line from composer to listener and about equidistant from west and east.

· Way down south, well below this line, we find his mirror image: the faithful student of the genius, the "disciple" who does not think for himself, who will not play a piece unless he has his master's fingerings. This rather gray attitude is quite frequently encountered in international competitions, but seldom among the prize-winners.

I have purposely sketched these four attitudes—east, west, north, south (as well as the distinction between amateur and professional musician)—in quite extreme degrees. Most performers intuitively take more moderate or mixed positions. However, choosing our position more consciously can open new possibilities.

c. Different Approaches to Early Music

Where does today's performer of Early Music stand in relation to this east-west line? As expected, we see a whole rainbow of different solutions co-existing; these are not so different from the attitudes I mentioned earlier.

- Some people behave as if nothing had happened in the field of Early Music since the 1950s. They stay untouched and uninterested by any historical information. They continue to use the modern instruments and the playing techniques and style that they inherited from their masters. In the best cases, they are up north, but otherwise they are rather down south and often quite west. In earlier decades they could often be heard stating that "historically informed" playing is, by its very nature, dull, absolutely east below the line, as if knowledge and scholarship were death blows to genuine musicianship. Fortunately this attitude is encountered less and less frequently.

- Other performers will still use modern instruments, but when they have to play earlier repertoire, they will listen to some recordings or take specialized coaching sessions. They do notice that performance traditions as well as audience's expectations are changing and do not want to miss the boat, but for whichever reason do not choose to invest very much time and energy in these changes and hesitate to go all the way in them. Generally they rely more on secondhand information than on direct personal investigation. Maybe their desire is to get a quick result, acceptable to many people: listeners, colleagues, concert series, orchestra managers. Unfortunately today many conductors and singers, even Early Music specialists, somehow also fall into this category. Though in theory, instrumentalists should learn

from the singers' example, singers often let someone else
—mostly an instrumentalist—apply an all too thin layer of
historical varnish upon their own fundamentally modern
base. If this kind of performer is of outstanding intrinsic
quality (well north), the result can be fascinating in its own
right, but the performer risks staying quite far from the
composer's east. If he is less captivating as an artist, he stays
just as far from the composer's east, but slides south.

· Some musicians are so fascinated by Early Music and all its
implications that they do invest a lot of time and effort; they
learn to play the old instruments, study the original sources,
and experience that historical performance practice is a
viable option. Where should we put them? Speaking from
my own experience and conviction, I would expect and hope
that learning to read the composer's language through his
own glasses can teach me to constantly redefine my position
according to era, genre, instrument, composer, composition,
concert venue, kind of audience, and, of course, my own
talent and temperament. In pieces where the structure seems
to be the main point, such as complicated fugues, I obviously
must stay east, very close to the composer, but the needs
of a charming French *Rondeau tendrement* will probably
put me west, closer to the audience. In a slow movement
of an *empfindsam* concerto, I should not hesitate to invent
elaborate ornamentations just like a true north prima donna.
Indeed, if the work has been conceived for that purpose,
I should fail ridiculously if I were to play or sing only the
notes of the Urtext edition in a completely east way! Even
within one single sonata (for example by Handel or one of his
contemporaries), I must usually change my position between
each movement. In the slow and extroverted first movement,
the tendency is north with a generous dose of "willkürliche
Veränderungen" and "wesentliche Manieren." The second
movement, often with active fugato writing, tends farther
east toward the composer. I need to stand more west in the
generally softer, introverted, and intimate third movement

(possibly a *siciliano* or a *dolce*); standing too far north there would make me feel out of place. For the final *giga* or other fast dance, I might want to stand upon or slightly above the line, pretty close to the audience, more west than east.

I must admit that I would not easily put myself below this east-west line, not even in a strict fugue. If I played only in the composer's name, without personal commitment and avoiding any contribution of my own, I would extinguish myself, and this would not place me in a good position to provide convincing communicative power. My playing should sound as if I just invented the piece myself. It should taste like freshly brewed coffee, not like yesterday's reheated leftovers.

16. EMOTION AND AFFECT

We all know and feel that in spoken language, the "real" meaning lies below or beyond the words. That is the benefit we receive by going to the theater, reading a book, or listening to poetry, by talking to somebody rather than writing. Because of the absence of text, the concepts and emotions represented in instrumental music could seem less specific. However, unspecified, unspoken, or unspeakable does not mean less strong or less real. Also in music, the meaning and emotions lie below the surface, beyond the notes. If we could express them by words, we might not need music.

Many texts about music or theater explain that you must be moved yourself if you wish to move your audience. In that respect, it strikes me that the word "emotion" (from the Latin "e[x]" = out of one place, and "movere" = to move) is so strongly connected to the body. We are "moved" indeed, put into motion out of one inner feeling into another. We are touched, transported, out of ourselves, captured, raptured, deafened, hurt, excited, breathless, caressed, aroused, or soothed— emotion is thus a physical state, not a theoretical concept.

Of course, if I were an opera singer, I must not really, personally, be in love with the heroine of the story, but I must feel as if I were. I definitely cannot see this as lying or pretending, nor would I consider it to be a sub-reality. It is rather a super-reality, as five-hundred-percent "real" as it can be for any little girl to "play" (but we all "play" music!) at being a princess. However, unlike the little girl, as a professional performer I do not play for myself, but for the audience.

Personal emotion and affect are not identical: I define affect as an organized emotion, which I have learned to recognize in the score.

It is an emotion that I truly and physically feel, but not for myself, not privately. I want to instill it into the audience. I borrow from the author the affect he designed and suggested, the affect he wants the audience to feel (it is also not their private or real-life emotion!). I accept it temporarily as my own, without reservation, even if it is at this moment foreign to me or to my cultural environment. For example, judging by the texts J. S. Bach used in his cantatas and passions, few people today would live and feel religion in the same way J. S. Bach did in his day. Nevertheless, I personally cannot imagine playing *"Aus Liebe will mein Heiland sterben"* from his St. Matthew Passion as if I were a complete atheist, without even momentarily striving to feel what moved Bach and his text author. For them, too, the chosen affect is what they wanted their audience to feel. Whether or not I am a Christian in my private life is none of the audience's business, but for the duration of that piece I must let the affect of that beautiful aria totally take possession of me—I must "truly" believe. When the performance is finished, I can give back to the composer what I had borrowed from him, feeling thoroughly grateful for the deep musical and spiritual experience.

Most listeners will experience these (changes of) affects unconsciously; they do not need an explanation. Similarly, a performing musician must not necessarily be able to identify each affect by its scientific name, provided he has learned to discern the affects in the compositions, and knows how to impart them toward the listener. I compare this to a medical drug—for me as consumer, it is more important that it is effective than that I know its name or the Latin enumeration of its components.

17. THE MIRROR

What "moves" into me from the score, through the affects staged by the author(s), will obviously stir my emotions. As an amateur I could keep these emotions to myself, but as a professional performer, I will direct the affects suggested by the composer (in as far as I can detect, accept, feel, and render them today) and my own momentaneous reactions to them together toward the audience. It is the peculiar balance between these two elements that makes each concert unique and worthwhile—the audience wants to hear, say, a particular J. S. Bach piece as it is understood by this or that artist. The listener will thus physically experience the composer's intentions only through my "translation"; I cannot possibly stay neutral. I call this transformation process within the performer the mirror effect.

Goethe, who as a playwright must have experienced this process from the point of view of the author, not of the performer, seems to be more restrictive. Among his many *Anweisungen für Schauspieler* (instructions for actors, collected during his tenure as theater director at Weimar between 1791 and 1817), there is reputed to be this one: "Der Interpret soll sein wie der Mond, der nur das Licht der Sonne wiedergibt" (The performer should be like the moon, which only reflects the light of the sun). If this is really authentic (which I have not been able to ascertain) he clearly and not very modestly identifies himself with the sun, and does not want the performer to take much personal initiative. However, in my opinion and experience as a performer, I must not even try to be personal or unique. I am, regardless. My mirror, which will reflect the "light" of the score, is handmade, with small errors and irregularities, with colored and blind spots. If I want my mirror to reflect a rich and complete image, I must let the score enter into me in all its broad and deep layers of meaning. Nothing can be reflected that was not captured by the mirror. I would certainly not position my mirror in front of myself, so that it stood between the score and me, but rather deep inside or even behind me. The image must fully penetrate and transpierce me, before I let it be reflected toward the audience.

After the performance, I can return to my actual, true self. After having reflected so many images, my mirror stays clean, limpid, unspoiled, unbroken, and ready for the next image.

As a practical consequence, it is obvious that my basic questions cannot be "What can I do with this piece?" or "Which interpretation should I construct?" or "Which ornamentation could I add?" I have to start with "What does this piece ask from me?" I do not want to read from my mind through my eyes and spectacles toward the score. As far as I am able to, I want to let the information given by the score jump into my eyes—but then I must keep my eyes, mind, spirit, heart, and body wide open, available, touchable, and vulnerable. If, on the contrary, I start from my own ambition and desire, from a perpetually north position, I risk pouring the same sauce (my "ketchup") over all the compositions I play. They might all end up tasting alike.

18. THE TWO-FOLD CONCEPT OF AUTHENTICITY

As a minimal sign of respect and responsibility toward both the composer and the audience, I feel I have to put together, accept, and apply all the existing evidence, as illustrated elsewhere in chapter 4. In my opinion this is no more than simply doing justice to the composer and his work, and taking both him and the listener seriously. By trying to assemble this giant jigsaw puzzle, I might approach some kind of a "Historical Authenticity." Sure enough, I am not so naïve as to expect to reach definitive answers and solutions. Given the constant changeability of art in performance, the "ultimate truth" might never have existed. However, besides the exterior facts and their interpretation leading to Historical Authenticity, I also need "Personal Authenticity." This is my emotional acceptance of the super-reality that I described in section 16. It is my personal contribution to the image that is mirrored, here and now, to the listener. Personal Authenticity also means I cannot and will not lie.

Both kinds of authenticity need and reinforce each other; each is insufficient and incomplete without the other. Even if I were a true north genius, my Personal Authenticity will remain limited, dry, and egotistical if it is not accompanied by Historical Authenticity. My emotional concepts need to be constantly questioned and ignited by the multiple layers of information and meaning handed down to me by the score and its contemporary performance conventions.

Conversely, without Personal Authenticity, I experience Historical Authenticity as pointless, hollow, insignificant, and dead. I would behave as if I had memorized the phonetics of a poem in an unknown language, without knowing and feeling what each word means, why the poet placed it exactly there, why the word has this particular form, which stress, accent, or pitch it receives, and what it could have meant to its author. I would feel ridiculous reciting, singing, or playing in this manner. If I were to do this as my regular job, I would—and should—be ashamed.

Only Historical Authenticity and Personal Authenticity together can give the listener both the message of the composer and its unique and honest reading by the performer, in ever-changing proportions. I do not see why the audience should get any less than that from us.

5

❧

OUTLOOK

❧

The notation gives us the raw but lifeless material from which we have to reinvent the actual music, applying the reading and performing conventions of different times and places. This quest will, of its nature, be a long one without easy, conclusive answers. It can continue to bear fruit if we stay close enough to the questions rather than to the answers. Some answers, though easy, tempting, fascinating, and fashionable, prove to be only temporary. They might blind us and lead us away from the essence of discovery. I am convinced that questions are more important and more interesting than answers. Over centuries humankind keeps asking the same questions; only the answers vary.

Sterility has been a fundamental criticism toward the Early Music movement because it appears to be more backward- than forward-looking. One cannot recreate the past, so the argument goes; therefore, it makes no sense to make the attempt. The argument continues to claim that historically informed Early Music performance is a typical late-twentieth-century phenomenon that says more about its practitioners than about the Early Music itself, and that it is condemned to failure in its attempt to reach its apparent goal. I can understand this criticism, but I would respond that no Early Music performer would be such a fool as to claim that he plays exactly like Bach or whomever

113

else. Only the worst commercial publicity for recordings or concerts will sometimes state this, and Early Music specialists should be the first to stop it.

Playing exactly like Bach is not my desire, and consequently I do not want to be accused of it. I try to understand Bach, or whatever other music I choose to play, with more and more insight. I do not want to bury the composer under my own sauce, or at least no more than he might sometimes have wished for or than what is inevitable anyway. I think that today's audience is not stupid, has an attention span longer than three minutes, does not need updated versions of old pieces, and is prepared to question traditions. Knowing and fully accepting that I cannot ever play like Bach—on which day of his life?—should not deter me from trying to move in his direction, from trying to get closer to him rather than farther away. I feel totally convinced that "the journey is more important than the goal." In this way, I do not believe that our generation should necessarily be "The End of Early Music," to quote the title of Bruce Haynes's last book. (The two of us had a wonderful exchange of ideas about it—with all respect, I often heartily disagreed—and I would have loved to further discuss it with him.) Certainly we and the next generations will have to remain active, alert, questioning, enterprising, inventive, creative, modest, honest . . . in order to remain personally as well as historically authentic.

Good luck!

SOURCES OF INSPIRATION

My vision of Early Music performance has received particularly stimulating impulses from many sides and on many occasions. I want to extend my heartfelt thanks to:

- Gustav Leonhardt: a unique blend of artistic integrity, superb musicianship, and knowledge.
- Alfred Deller: an inimitable voice, with true expressive power and great diction.
- My brothers Sigiswald and Wieland, and Robert Kohnen: wonderful companions in many concerts and recordings, partners in discussion and discovery.
- La Petite Bande: the orchestra where I could put into practice what I had learned.
- The many historical recordings of famous singers, violinists, pianists, flautists . . .
- Frans Vester: an original and inquiring mind, an eye-opening and ear-opening teacher, as well as a provocative one.
- My students, who teach me so much.
- My good old Godefroy Adrien Rottenburgh flute, which showed me the way to go.
- Andreas Glatt, Rudolf Tutz, Alain Weemaels, Rod Cameron: wonderful instrument makers who have provided me with

beautiful flutes and with whom I can discuss historical flute making and share workshop experiences.

· The Brussels Musical Instrument Museum and many private owners of historical instruments: the hands-on studying, playing, and measuring of so many old flutes and recorders has been an invaluable help.

· The record label Accent and its founders Andreas and Adelheid Glatt: I was invited to record the major works of the flute repertoire until ca. 1840, which led me to focus on them and research them in theory and practice, at my own pace.

· The library of the Brussels Royal Conservatory, where I go treasure-hunting and where I learnt to know not only the masterworks of a period but also the average and below-average works of composers.

· Museums, palaces, and churches all over the world, which enabled me to see music in context with the other arts.

BIBLIOGRAPHY

Many old and new writings have helped me enormously in finding my way. The following list is not exhaustive—it is the tip of the iceberg. At the same time it is a selected bibliography of this essay. If I do not mention some older or more recently published studies, this means that, though interesting, important, and valuable, they have not significantly changed the direction of my approach. Consulting the original sources usually gives me a deeper and broader perspective.

PRIMARY SOURCES

Agricola, Johann Friedrich and Pier Francesco Tosi. *Anleitung zur Singkunst.* Berlin: 1757.

———. *"Georg Simon Löhleins Clavier-Schule."* In *Allgemeine deutsche Bibliothek.* Berlin: 1769. See also *Bach-Dokumente III.* Kassel and New York: 1963.

Bach, Carl Philipp Emanuel. *Versuch über die wahre Art das Clavier zu spielen.* Berlin: 1753 (part I) and 1762 (part II). The editions of 1784 (part I) and 1797 (part II) include new material.

———. *Sonaten mit veränderten Reprisen.* Berlin: 1760.

———. Autobiographie, in Carl Burney's *"Der Musik Doctors Tagebuch seiner musikalischen Reisen,"* vol. 3, *Durch Böhmen, Sachsen, Brandenburg, Hamburg und Holland.* Hamburg: 1773.

Bacilly, Bénigne de. *Remarques curieuses sur l'Art de bien Chanter.* Paris: 1668.

Bagatella, Antonio. *Regole per la costruzione de' violini viole violoncelli e violoni.* Padova: 1786.

Beethoven, Ludwig van. *Johann Baptist Cramer: 21 Etüden nebst Fingerübungen von Beethoven nach seinem Handexemplar.* Edited by Hans Kann. Wien: 1974.

Brahms, Johannes. "Correspondence with Joseph Joachim." In Clive Brown, 1999.

Bremner, Robert. *Some Thoughts on the Performance of Concert Music.* (Preface to his publication of J. G. C. Schetky's *6 Quartettos* opus 6.) Edinburgh: 1777. See also Geminiani, 1751.

Burney, Charles. *Music, Men and Manners in France and Italy.* MS, 1770. London: 1969.

―――. *The Present State of Music in France and Italy.* London: 1771, 2/1773.

―――. *The Present State of Music in Germany, The Netherlands, and United Provinces.* London: 1773, 2/1775.

Caruso, Enrico and Luisa Tetrazzini. *Caruso and Tetrazzini on the Art of Singing.* New York: 1909.

Corrette, Michel: *l'Ecole d'Orphée. Méthode pour apprendre facilement à jouer du violon dans le goût françois et italien.* Paris: 1738.

―――. *Methode théorique et pratique pour apprendre en peu de tems le violoncelle dans sa perfection.* Paris: 1741.

―――. *Methode pour apprendre aisément à jouer de la flute traversiere.* Paris: ca. 1742.

―――. *Methode pour apprendre facilement à jouer du pardessus de viole.* Paris: 1748.

―――. *l'art de se perfectionner dans le Violon.* Paris: 1782.

Corri, Domenico, ed. *A Select Collection of the Most Admired Songs, Duets Etc. From Operas in the Highest Esteem.* 5 vols. London: 1780–1810.

Couperin, François. *l'art de Toucher le Clavecin.* Paris: 1717.

―――. "Preface." In *Pieces de Clavecin.* Paris: 1713.

Crescentini, Girolamo. *Venti Cinque Solfeggi Variati Per Esercitare La Voce a Vocalizzare.* Paris: between 1819 and 1828.

Darwin, Charles. *On the Origin of Species by Means of Natural Selection, or, the Preservation of Favoured Races in the Struggle for Life.* London: 1859, 2/1872.

Delusse, Charles. *l'art de la flûte traversiere.* Paris: 1761.

Falck, Georg. *Idea Boni Cantoris.* Nürnberg: 1688.

Fétis, François-Joseph. *Biographie universelle des musiciens et bibliographie générale de la musique.* Bruxelles: 1835–1844, 2/1860–1865.

Fürstenau, Anton Bernhard. *Die Kunst des Flötenspiels.* Leipzig: 1844.

Geminiani, Francesco. *The Art of Playing on the Violin.* London: 1751, 2/ed. Robert Bremner. London: 1777.

―――. *A Treatise of Good Taste in the Art of Music.* London: 1749.

―――. *Rules for Playing in a True Taste on the Violin German Flute Violoncello and Harpsichord Particularly the Thorough Bass, op. 8.* London: ca. 1748.

Gluck, Christoph Willibald von. "Preface." In *Alceste.* Wien: 1769.

―――. "Preface." In *Elena e Paride.* Wien: 1770.

Goethe, Johann Wolfgang von. *Begegnungen und Gespräche, vol. 6.* Berlin and New York: 1999.

Grétry, André Ernest Modeste. *Mémoires ou essays sur la musique.* Paris: 1789–1797, 2/1812.

Hotteterre le Romain, Jacques. *Principes de la flute traversiere.* Paris: 1707.

―――. *l'art de Préluder.* Paris: 1719.

l'Affilard, Michel. *Principes très faciles pour bien apprendre la Musique.* Paris: 1705.

Loulié, Étienne. *Élements ou Principes de Musique.* Paris: 1696.

Mattheson, Johann. *Kern melodischer Wissenschaft.* Hamburg: 1737.

―――. *Der vollkommene Capellmeister.* Hamburg: 1739.

Mermet, Louis Bollioud de. *De la corruption du goust dans la musique françoise.* Lyon: 1746.

Mozart, Leopold. *Versuch einer gründlichen Violinschule.* Augsburg: 1756.

Mozart, Wolfgang Amadeus. *Briefe und Aufzeichnungen.* Kassel and New York: 1962–1975.

Muffat, Georg. "Preface." In *Armonico tributo.* Salzburg: 1682.

———. "Preface." In *Florilegium Primum.* Augsburg: 1695.

———. "Preface." In *Florilegium secundum.* Passau: 1698.

Nivers, Guillaume Gabriel. "Preface." In *Livre d'Orgue Contenant Cent Pièces de tous les Tons de l'Eglise.* Paris: 1665.

North, Roger. Extracts of his writings. In *Roger North on Music.* Ed. John Wilson, London: 1959.

Quantz, Johann Joachim. *Solfeggi pour la flute traversiere avec l'enseignement.* MS, DK-Kk, n.d. Winterthur: 1978.

———. *Versuch einer Anweisung die Flöte traversiere zu spielen.* Berlin, 1752.

———. *Herrn Johann Joachim Quantzens Lebenslauf, von ihm selbst entworfen.* In Fr. W. Marpurg: *Historisch-kritische Beyträge zur Aufnahme der Musik.* Berlin: 1755, vol. 1, Stück 3. Münster: 1997.

Reichardt, Johann Friedrich. *Briefe eines aufmerksamen Reisenden, die Musik betreffend.* Vol. 1: Frankfurt and Leipzig, 1774. Vol. 2: Frankfurt and Breslau: 1776.

Riemann, Hugo. *Musikalische Dynamik Und Agogik. Lehrbuch Der Musikalischen Phrasirung Auf Grund Einer Revision Der Lehre Von Der Musikalischen Metrik und Rhythmik.* Hamburg: 1884.

———. *System Der Musikalischen Rhythmik Und Metrik.* Leipzig: 1903.

Scheibe, Johann Adolf. *Der Critische Musikus.* Hamburg: 1738–40.

Schoenberg, Arnold. "Preface." In *Pierrot Lunaire.* Wien: 1914.

Spencer, Herbert. *Principles of Biology.* London: 1864.

Spohr, Louis. *Selbstbiographie.* 2 Vol. Kassel: 1860–61.

Stravinsky, Igor. "Some Ideas about my Octuor." In *The Arts,* January 1924.

Tartini, Giuseppe. *Traité des Agréments de la Musique.* Paris: 1771.

Telemann, Georg Philipp. "Preface." In *Harmonischer Gottes-Dienst, Oder Geistliche Cantaten Zum Allgemeinen Gebrauche.* Hamburg: 1725–26.

Tromlitz, Johann Georg. *Ausführlicher und gründlicher Unterricht die Flöte zu spielen.* Leipzig: 1791.

———. *Ueber die Flöte mit mehrern Klappen.* Leipzig: 1800.

Walther, Johann Gottfried. *Praecepta der musikalischen Composition.* MS, 1708. Leipzig: 1955.

———. *Musicalisches Lexicon.* Leipzig: 1732.

Wieck, Friedrich. *Clavier und Gesang, Didaktisches und Polemisches.* Leipzig: 1853.

SECONDARY SOURCES

Bach, Johann Sebastian. *Sonate für Flöte und Cembalo A-dur BWV 1032.* Edited and reconstructed by Barthold Kuijken. Wiesbaden: 1997.

Brown, Clive. *Classical & Romantic Performance Practice 1750–1900.* Oxford: 1999.

Brown, Howard Mayer, and Stanley Sadie, eds. *Performance Practice.* 2 vols. The Norton/Grove Handbooks in Music. New York: 1990.

Byrt, John. "Elements of rhythmic inequality in the arias of Alessandro Scarlatti and Handel." In *Early Music* 35, no. 4 (November 2007): 609–627.

———. "Inequality in Alessandro Scarlatti and Handel: A Sequel." In *Early Music* 40, no. 1 (February 2012): 91–110.

Craft, Robert. *Conversations with Igor Stravinsky.* New York: 1959.

Demeyere, Ewald. *Johann Sebastian Bach's Art of Fugue: Performance Practice Based on German Eighteenth-Century Theory.* Publication scheduled 2013, Leuven.

Dolmetsch, Arnold. *The Interpretation of the Music of the XVIIth and XVIIIth Centuries Revealed by Contemporary Evidence.* London: 1915.

Donington, Robert. *The Interpretation of Early Music.* New York: 1965.

Eppstein Hans. *Studien über J. S. Bachs Sonaten für ein Melodieinstrument und obligates Cembalo.* Uppsala: 1966.

Geoffroy-Dechaume, Antoine. *Les 'Secrets' de la musique ancienne.* Paris: 1964.

Gérold, Théodore. *l'art du chant en France au XVIIième siècle.* Strasbourg: 1921.

Haynes, Bruce. *The Eloquent Oboe.* New York: 2001.

———. *A History of Performing Pitch: The Story of "A."* Lanham, Md.: 2002.

———. *The End of Early Music.* New York: 2007.

Hefling, Stephen. *Rhythmic Alteration in Seventeenth- and Eighteenth-Century Music.* New York: 1993.

Hudson, Richard. *Stolen Time: The History of Tempo Rubato.* Oxford: 1994.

Lindley, Mark. "Tuning and Intonation." In Howard Mayer Brown and Stanley Sadie, 1990.

Maunder, Richard. *The Scoring of Baroque Concertos.* Woodbridge: 2004.

Mengelberg, Willem. "St. Matthew Passion." In *Columbia Masterworks,* 1939.

Miehling, Klaus. *Das Tempo in der Musik von Barock und Vorklassik: die Antwort der Quellen auf ein umstrittenes Thema.* "Heinrichshofen Bücher." Wilhelmshaven: 1993.

Parrott, Andrew. *The Essential Bach Choir.* Woodbridge, UK, and Rochester, NY: 2000.

Potter, John. "Reconstructing Lost Voices," in Tess Knighton and David Fallows, *Companion to Medieval and Renaissance Music.* Oxford: 1997. 311–316.

———. "The Tenor-Castrato Connection." In *Early Music* 35, no. 1 (February 2007): 97–110.

Schwarzkopf, Elisabeth. *On and Off the Record: A Memoir of Walter Legge.* New York: 1982.

Smith, Anne. *The Performance of 16th-Century Music: Learning from the Theorists.* New York: 2011.

Spitta, Philipp. *Johann Sebastian Bach.* Leipzig: 1873–1880.

Spitzer, John and Neal Zaslaw. *The Birth of the Orchestra: History of an Institution.* Oxford and New York: 2004.

Zaslaw, Neal. *Mozart's Symphonies. Context, Performance Practice, Reception.* Oxford: 1989.

———. "Ornaments for Corelli's violin sonatas, op.5." In *Early Music* 24, no. 1 (February 1996): 95–115.

Zwang, Gérard. *Guide pratique des Cantates de Bach.* Paris: 1982.

———. *Le Diapason.* Paris: 1998.

JOURNALS

Bach-Jahrbuch (Leipzig)
Early Music (Oxford)
Performance Practice Review (Madison)
Tibia (Celle)

WEBSITES

www.bach-digital.de
www.imslp.org
www.loc.gov/jukebox/

SELECTIVE INDEX

This index references the most relevant composers and concepts.
Page numbers in italics refer to illustrations.

CONCEPTS

affect, 107–12
amateur, 66, 100–101, 109
arrangement, 65–66, 68–71
articulation, 8, 13, 32, 48, 52–55, 77
artistic experience, moment of, 14
audience, attitude of, 97–99
authenticity, 10, 111–114

basso continuo, 73–75

cadenza, 85–88
choir, 29, 61, 62, 63
compass, 101–104, *102*
compromise, 22, 23, 24, 58, 70
conductor, absence or presence, 12, 62, 63
contradictions, 7–8

difference tone, 31
double, 83
dynamics, 9, 13, 32, 48, 53, 54, 56–60

editions, 8, 13, 65, 80, 91–94, 103, 105
emotion, 8, 14, 77, 79, 107–12

flute, Godefroy Adrien Rottenburgh, 6, 20

good and bad notes, 42, 51, 55, 56–57
good taste, 2, 14, 38, 41, 47, 65, 77, 78, 83–84

historical recordings, 9, 13, 14–15, 33, 53, 57, 58, 62–63, 80

improvisation, 88, 89
inequality, 39–44, 45, 49, 56
instrumentation, 3, 63–66, 73, 75, 91, 93

mirror, 109–111

ornamentation, 13, 32, 42, 54, 72, 76–84, 91, 105
orchestra, 12, 13, 31, 40, 58, 59, 60, 61, 62, 63, 77
overdotting, 44, 45

pedagogy, 3, 4, 6, 7, 8, 10, 93–94
performance practice, criticism on, 2–3, 38, 44, 50, 55, 59, 70–71, 73–74, 75, 77, 78, 79, 83, 84, 87, 104–105, 113–14
performer's: addition to notation, 1, 2, 9, 14; annotations in part or score, 13, 77; attitude, 100–114
phrasing, 8, 32, 48, 49–51, 55
pitch, 7, 19–24, 29
poetic feet, 39, 40, 51, 56
progress, 68, 69

reading: creative, 9; decoded, 12, 87; literal, 1–2, 8, 11–12, 45
reconstruction, J. S. Bach, BWV 1032, 66–68
research, artistic, xi–xii, 4, 5–10
rhetoric, 32, 48, 52–53
rhythm, 32, 39–47, 53, 82
rubato, 3, 9, 15, 36–38, 78, 80

singing, 9, 15, 19, 21, 28, 36, 39–41, 42–43, 50–58, 61, 62, 63, 70, 77–80, 82–83, 85–86, 93, 98, 100, 104–105, 107, 112
score, absence or presence, 12–13

temperament and intonation, 7, 18, 20, 23, 26–31, 78
tempo, 9, 32–36, 44, 50, 80, 84, 85

underdotting, 44, 45

vibrato, 3, 53, 54, 57, 77–79

World-renowned baroque flautist, conductor, and researcher Dr. Barthold Kuijken is considered one of the pioneers of the Early Music movement. As Professor of baroque flute at the Royal Conservatories of The Hague and Brussels (where he is also Head of the Early Music Section), he teaches that music of the past is rendered best when performed on original instruments, using appropriate performance practices. An autodidact of historical flutes, Barthold Kuijken's recordings of the baroque, classical, and romantic flute repertory are universally acclaimed.

CPSIA information can be obtained
at www.ICGtesting.com
Printed in the USA
BVOW03*1826141217
502818BV00002B/5/P